A COOK'S INITIATION INTO THE GORGEOUS WORLD OF MUSHROOMS

ACKNOWLEDGMENTS

Thanks to my mom and my Aunt Lisette for having given me my love of cooking, and thanks to Linette for nourishing it every day. Thanks to Fred for the great job and for the team at MOTO that I didn't manage. Thank you to Pierre for the initiation, and a special dedication to all of my friends who participated in the experiment of Café des Spores (*indoor* and *outdoor*). I will never finish thanking Diego, Cecile, Eugenie, Cedric, Joel, Sara, Maria, Emilia, Faika, Sabrina, Natasha, Naima, Jeremi, David, and Thierry. And finally thank you to Pascal, our plumber, and Paolo (refrigeration), without whom it all would have been a disaster.

A special thank you to Myrto, who masterfully plays all roles at once, and to Fotis for opening so many channels for me.

CAFÉ DES SPORES
BRUXELLES, PAS PARIS, PAS NEW YORK,
PAS LONDRES, PAS TOKYO, PAS MADRID,
NI LE ZOUTE, NI MILAN, NI SAINT-TROPEZ

First published in the United States of America in 2013 by Chronicle Books LLC.
First published in France in 2011 by Marabout.

Library of Congress Cataloging-in-Publication Data available.

ISBN 978-1-4521-1445-3

Manufactured in China

Designed by MOTO
Typesetting by DC Typography, Inc.

10 9 8 7 6 5 4 3 2 1

Chronicle Books LLC
680 Second Street
San Francisco, California 94107
www.chroniclebooks.com

A COOK'S INITIATION INTO THE GORGEOUS WORLD OF MUSHROOMS

Philippe Emanuelli

Photographs by Frédéric Raevens
Translated by Martha Holmberg

CHRONICLE BOOKS
SAN FRANCISCO

My goal in writing this book was to introduce you to the pleasures of cooking with mushrooms, which is something I've been experimenting with over the last few years. The book is definitely not an exhaustive survey of all the edible mushrooms, but rather a selection of the ones I find most often on display in the markets of Europe, both in the city and the countryside. In no way is this book meant to encourage you to do your own mushroom hunting.

- Unless you are highly experienced, gathering and eating wild mushrooms is VERY dangerous—so dangerous that even pharmacists aren't trained in mushroom identification anymore (as was traditional for so many years in Europe).

- The environments in which mushrooms grow are becoming more and more fragile, and thus more and more precious. In the United States, the harvesting of many types of mushrooms is monitored and managed with land and species conservation in mind. And yet, the interest in mushroom foraging is, well, mushrooming. This sometimes puts the casual Sunday mushroom hunter at odds with local environmentalists and federal regulators, and makes something as seemingly natural as hunting for mushrooms an affront to true nature lovers.
And foraging on your own can impinge on the livelihood of others. Some regions of the world have active mushroom foraging cultures that make important contributions to the local economy, both socially and environmentally.

- Nowadays, plenty of markets—especially farmers' markets—offer a wonderful variety of high-quality, well-handled, safe-to-eat wild mushrooms, so why not just leave it to the experts to do the foraging?

I also encourage you to eat more cultivated mushrooms. They're less expensive, less apt to be polluted, often organic, widely available, ready to cook, and wholesome and nutritious—plenty of good reasons why they're finding their way to so many urban kitchens and pantries.

Now, in spite of everything I've just said, if you can't resist the lure of the mushroom hunt, here is some useful advice:

- Even if it means a long hike, don't park your car near secret (or even well-known) foraging sites, especially if your car betrays you as being not local—flat tires and scratched paint jobs are pretty much guaranteed. Be discreet and respectful. For example, only take what you will eat, and don't leave any signs of your visit.

- Must-have items: cell phone, watch, a good mushroom field guide, good walking shoes.

- Never put your mushrooms in a plastic bag or pouch; certain species become toxic if sealed in plastic.

- Never taste any mushroom that you're not absolutely certain about, and even then, only taste a bit.

- As a way to curb any reckless behavior, take a look at the list of mushroom poisoning symptoms. That'll do the trick! And be sure to program the poison-control-center phone number into your cell phone.

CONTENTS

ABOUT MUSHROOMS

DEFINITION OF A MUSHROOM: All mushrooms share the common trait of containing no chlorophyll (green pigmentation), which is one thing that distinguishes them from more complex vegetables. This means they are incapable of synthesizing the essential products of photosynthesis (sugars, starches), and therefore they need to get these elements from other organisms (vegetal and animal) on which they are dependent.

The visible fleshy portion, which is what we eat, is simply the fruit of the mushroom, which actually lives underground as a complex network of microscopic filaments, called the mycelium. These filaments grow in different ways: they either make use of the surrounding dead organic matter (leaf humus, compost) or live organic matter (trees and plants), or they develop a symbiotic relationship with a living organism, usually a tree or plant. In this case, the expanding network surrounds the tiny roots and creates what's called a mycorrhiza, like a little biological factory that's beneficial to both organisms. The mushroom captures water and minerals for its host and creates antibiotics, and, in exchange, the host provides the organic matter the mushroom needs to consume. Porcini, chanterelles, and truffles all use this same process.

SEASONS: Contrary to what most people think, mushrooms don't only grow in the fall. They start appearing as soon as the snow melts and they grow all the way through the next winter, with a slow season from April to November. And the seasons are flexible, given that mushrooms grow in so many climates around the world. And don't forget, cultivated and dried mushrooms are available year-round.

COMPOSITION: Mushrooms contain proteins (similar to animal protein), vitamins, and various minerals—all in relatively small amounts, however, because mushrooms are about 90 percent water. Dried mushrooms, therefore, have much higher levels of these nutrients.

In spite of their nutritional value—and their popularity with food lovers—mushrooms can have certain health risks. As with shellfish, mushrooms have the tendency to absorb pollutants (pesticides, heavy metals, radioactivity). This is especially true for certain "at risk" varieties and wild varieties growing in unprotected areas (grasslands, fallow farm fields, country lanes, and areas bordering conventionally farmed, nonorganic fields). This isn't so different from the vast majority of fruits and vegetables these days, which also contain pollutants.

Here are a few precautions you can take: 1) Avoid the riskiest wild varieties (agarics, for example). 2) Eat wild mushrooms in moderate quantities, no more than 5 to 7 oz a day. 3) Don't hesitate to eat as many cultivated mushrooms as you like, especially organic ones.

A lot of cultivated mushrooms are being studied for their therapeutic properties. Long recognized for their curative value in traditional medicine, especially Chinese, Japanese, and Korean cultures, many mushrooms are thought to have amazing properties, such as immune boosting, antibiotic, cholesterol reducing, blood thinning, and more.

ANTICARCINOGENIC
BETA-GLUCANS
CHOLESTEROL-LOWERING
GOOD SOURCE OF SELENIUM
GOOD SOURCE OF VITAMINS A AND D
IMMUNE-SUPPORTING
LINOLEIC ACID
LIVER FUNCTION–BOOSTING
MINERALS
NATURAL INSULIN SOURCE
PROTEINS
VIRUS-INHIBITING

NICOLETTA DIASIO anthropolog

« Ce qui

Nicoletta Diasio, anthropolo-
gue (1), est l'une des directri-
ces scientifiques du projet de
recherche AlimAdos.

**Votre discours sur l'alimentation des
ados paraît beaucoup plus détendu
que ce que l'on entend d'ordinaire ?**
En confrontant le discours ambi
aux pratiques réelles, no
sommes aperçus que l'
adolescence et malbou
Certes, il y a dans le
des hamburgers, d
zas, mais seuleme
la réalité, les situ
ment variées que
est très diversifiée
d'ailleurs, on peut
tronomie adolesce
**A quoi ressemble cet
adolescente» ?**
C'est une recherche du go

LITTLE LEXICON
OF BASICS

AMOUNTS: In these recipes, we're using 3.5 to 6 oz per person of trimmed and cleaned fresh mushrooms. To figure the starting weight that you need to buy, add about 20 percent to wild mushrooms and 10 percent to cultivated ones.

Truffles are a separate case; given their astronomic prices as well as the intensity of their flavor, you'll only need to count on 0.35 to 1 oz per person.

For dried mushrooms, the price will be much higher per pound than its fresh counterpart because, while the drying process increases the mushroom's flavor and nutritional value (the protein content), it also reduces its weight. In our recipes, we're using a maximum of about 0.75 oz per person.

BRUSH: This is the simplest and most efficient way to remove any bits of soil, leaves, or moss that may be clinging to the mushrooms. Choose a supple, soft brush, and try to avoid synthetic bristles.

BUGS: You can tell whether a mushroom is wormy by checking the stem (split the end of the stem lengthwise and take a look). Most of the time, you'll find some insect larvae, white and wriggling and not at all appetizing. If they're close to the cap, let the mushrooms rest cap-side down overnight: the larvae will move up the stem away from the cap, so you can then cut off the ends and discard them. With porcini, if the stem is slightly infested, split the stems lengthwise, arrange the mushrooms split-side down on a rack set over a piece of newspaper, and leave overnight (it doesn't have to be a full moon, either!).

Mushrooms that have a hollow stem can also shelter a few little guests, often wood lice or little slugs. Examine the stems and then use the tip of your knife to encourage them to vacate. If you miss a slug, you'll find it easily on your dinner plate (they turn blue when cooked!).

CUTICLE: This is the thin membrane that covers the fleshy cap of most gilled mushrooms as well as porcini. There's no need to remove it, unless the mushrooms are very dirty (as with russulas) or slimy (as with some porcini). To remove it, scrape it off with the point of a knife.

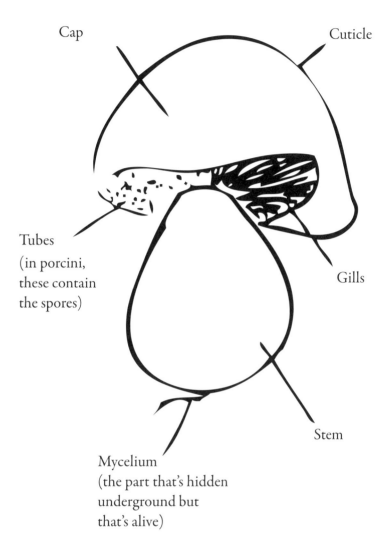

Cap

Cuticle

Tubes
(in porcini,
these contain
the spores)

Gills

Stem

Mycelium
(the part that's hidden
underground but
that's alive)

FAT: Indispensable for releasing and carrying flavor, fat should be used in moderation and with attention paid to the type you choose. We prefer fats that can withstand high heat and contain the least amount of saturated fat as possible: goose fat, clarified butter, grapeseed oil, and lard. Whole butter burns at 250°F, making it taste toxic and unpleasant. But once the milk solids have been removed, clarified butter (see the method on page 18) becomes stable and able to withstand high cooking temperatures (over 400°F). This is similar to Indian ghee. When cooking mushrooms, it's best to start off at high temperature, which prevents the water from seeping out and making the mushrooms soggy; the exterior of the mushrooms fries and caramelizes, while the inside becomes tender. We do, however, sometimes toss in a chunk of butter right at the end, off the heat, so that it melts but doesn't actually cook. The flavor is irreplaceable.

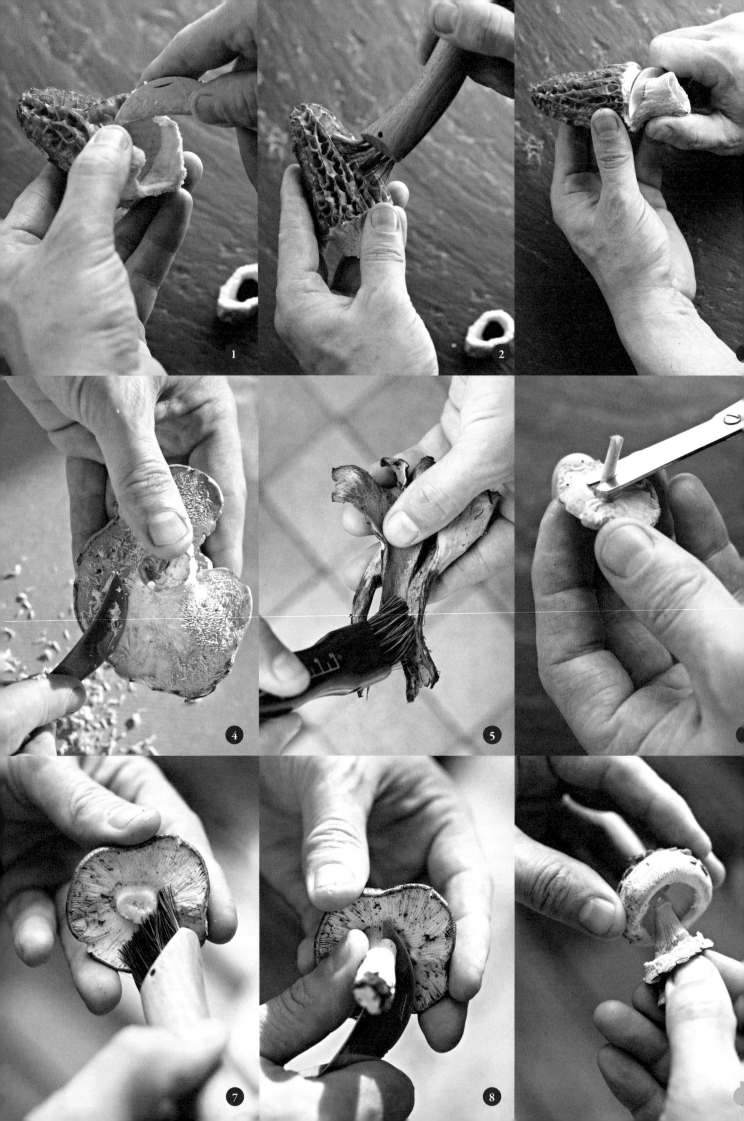

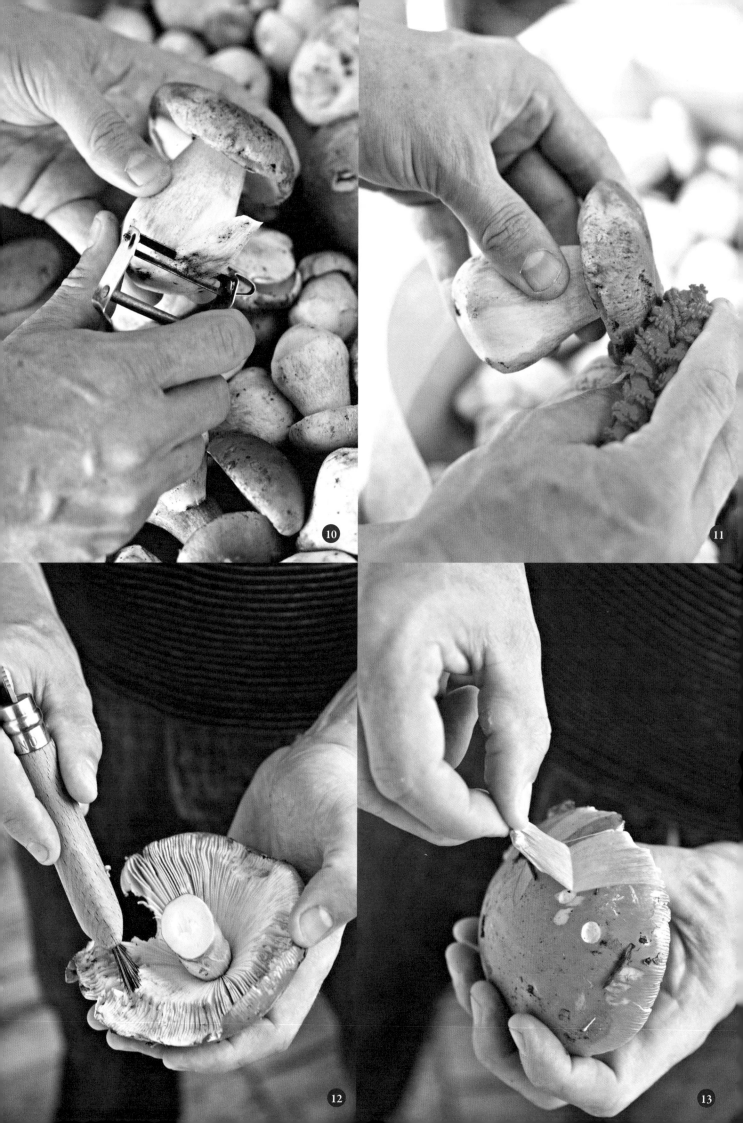

10

11

12

13

Clarifying butter at home is simple. Put a stick or two of butter in a ovenproof bowl, put the bowl in a low oven (200°F) or on a warm radiator. As it melts, the milk protein, called casein (the milky white solids), will separate from the butterfat (the clear yellow liquid). Carefully pour off the butterfat to use and discard the milk solids. Goose fat is also great to cook with, and its flavor is a perfect partner for certain mushrooms (porcini, chanterelles).

Lard has interesting properties in the kitchen, but it can give a slightly off taste to mushrooms, though it pairs well with black trumpet mushrooms. Grapeseed oil is good for frying, alone or mixed with peanut oil. Olive oil pairs well with chanterelles, but we generally only use it in uncooked dishes. Same goes with other specialty oils, especially hazelnut or walnut oil.

GARLIC: Despite what many people think, garlic isn't used that often in mushroom cookery. Its aggressive flavor and fragrance mean it's not always a great partner (other than in a classic *persillade*—see Herbs, following). When you do use garlic, follow these tips to get the best results: If you don't have very fresh, spring garlic, split the clove and flick out the small green germ you may find in the center; this will make the garlic easier to digest. Blanch the cloves once or twice in boiling water before using. Don't add garlic early on in the cooking, because it burns easily at high temperatures; only add the garlic about halfway through cooking.

HERBS: *Persillade* (parsley and garlic) is to mushrooms as tartar sauce is to fish and chips—a classic combination—but of course plenty of other herbs are delicious with mushrooms. Here are some good pairings: white mushrooms with chives, agarics with tarragon, bluefoots with sage, chanterelles with basil, milky caps with thyme, morels with savory, fairy rings with ramps. But let's give props to parsley, too, and talk technique—you add the washed, dried, and chopped parsley to the mushroom dishes in two stages. First, add about half your parsley halfway through cooking, so it infuses its flavor into the dish, cooks down a bit, and in some cases fries along with porcini, for example. Then add the rest of the parsley at the end of cooking, which lends a hit of freshness to the final dish.

KNIFE: There are specially designed mushroom-cleaning knives, useful both in the forest and the kitchen. The blade is short and slightly curving and a brush extends from the end of the handle, usually boar bristle; sometimes they even include tweezers for picking off pine needles. A good substitute is a nice paring knife or a utility knife such as an Opinel. A vegetable peeler is also useful. You need a special tool for truffles, a sort of tiny mandoline with an adjustable blade so you can control the thickness of your slices.

MOUSSE (OR TUBES): This is the soft, beige-to-light-green substance found on the underside of a porcini cap. It's made up of tiny tubes that house the mushroom spores. On older, very opened specimens, it's best to scrape this off before cooking because the mousse can be unpleasant and slightly bitter, as well as hard to digest, since it soaks up the cooking fat.

SALT: Always salt at the end of cooking, not at the start of the process. The salt will draw out the moisture from the mushrooms through osmosis and make it difficult to cook them properly.

STEM: The stem will be different with every type of mushroom. Porcini or white mushroom stems are delicious, meatier, and sweeter even than the caps; you simply need to peel the base of the stem, which can be gritty, using a vegetable peeler. The stems of stringier mushrooms, such as black trumpets and chanterelles, are ridged and often full of bits of soil: just pinch them off with your fingers. Other mushrooms have fibrous stems that need to be removed (parasol mushrooms, fairy rings). And some mushrooms—namely truffles—don't have stems at all, so dealing with their stems isn't an issue.

WATER: The texture of mushrooms can be ruined by water, making them bland and difficult to brown properly. In some cases, however, you'll need to wash your mushrooms, for example with morels, which can be quite sandy, or with craggy, crenellated mushrooms, such as black trumpet or chanterelle.

To wash, dunk them quickly in a bowl of water mixed with a bit of vinegar (this will encourage any critters to leave). Dry them immediately. For very fragile varieties (morels, cauliflower mushrooms), gently blot dry with a kitchen towel. For stringier, tougher varieties, dry them in a salad spinner.

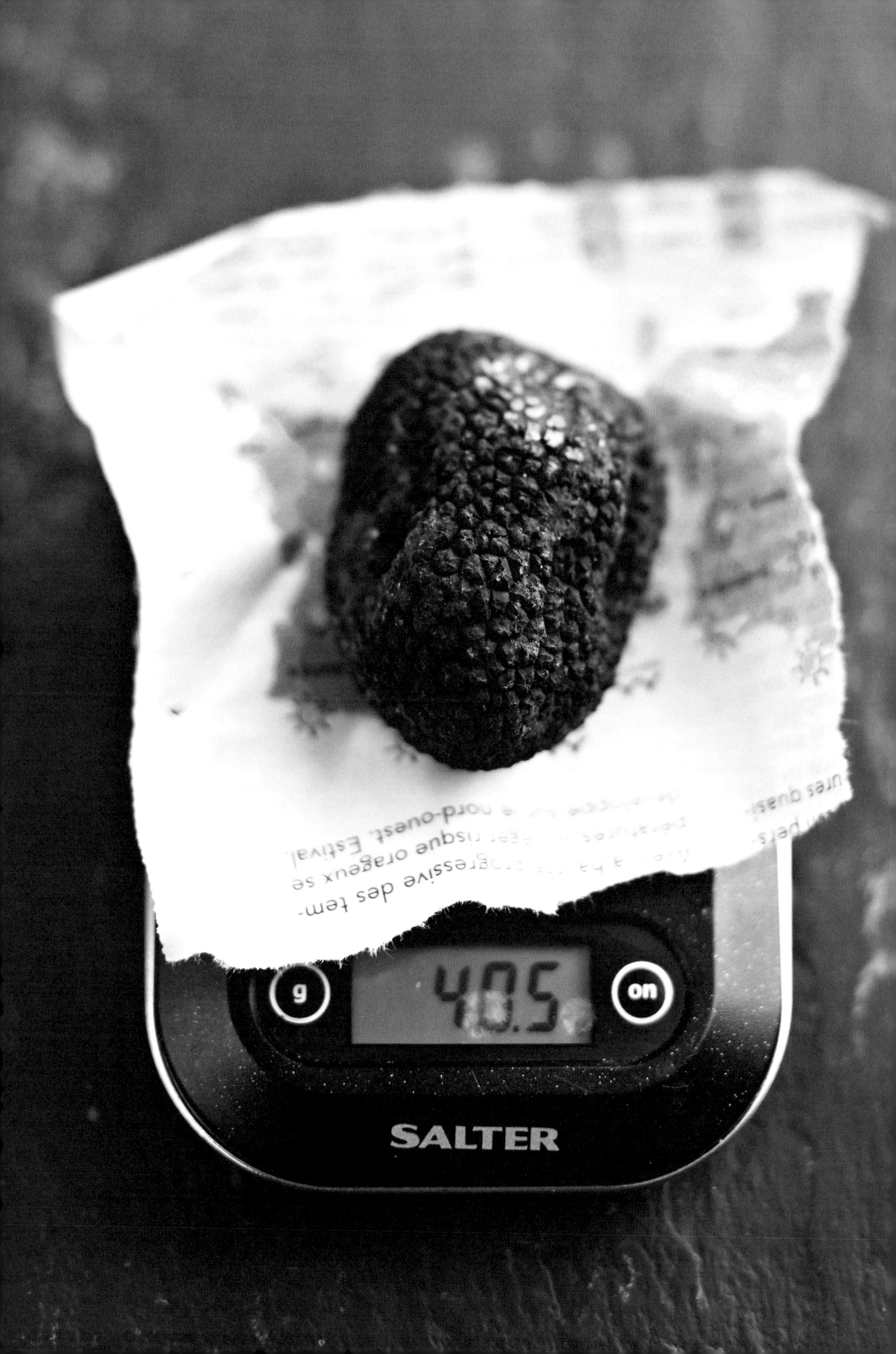
g
40.5
on
SALTER

RECIPE INDEX

VISUAL
INDEX
OF
MUSHROOMS

MOREL
MORCHELLA ESCULENTA
(MARCH ▸ MAY)

FAIRY RING
MARASMIUS OREADES
(MAY ▸ SEPTEMBER)

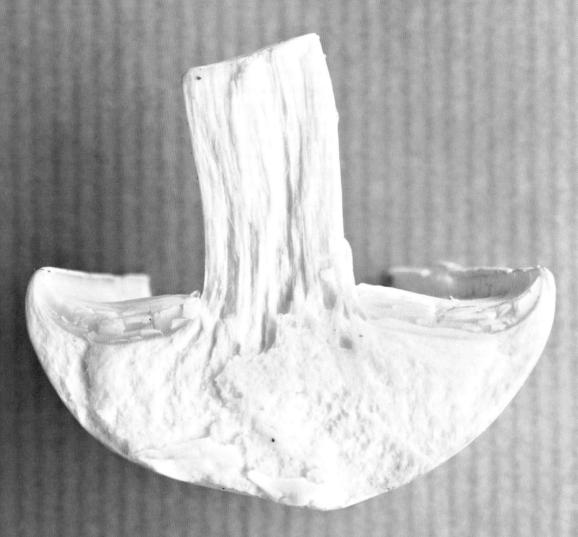

ST. GEORGE'S MUSHROOM
CALOCYBE GAMBOSA
(APRIL ► JUNE)

CHANTERELLE
CANTHARELLUS CIBARIUS
(JUNE ▸ NOVEMBER)

SUMMER TRUFFLE
TUBER AESTIVUM
(JUNE ▸ SEPTEMBER)

CAESAR'S MUSHROOM
AMANITA CAESAREA
(JULY ▸ OCTOBER)

HEDGEHOG MUSHROOM
HYDNUM REPANDUM
(JUNE ▸ NOVEMBER)

PORCINI
BOLETUS EDULIS
(JULY ▸ OCTOBER)

BLACK TRUMPET
CRATERELLUS
CORNUCOPIOIDES
(SEPTEMBER ► DECEMBER)

PARASOL MUSHROOM
MACROLEPIOTA PROCERA
(AUGUST ▸ OCTOBER)

CAULIFLOWER MUSHROOM
SPARASSIS CRISPA
(AUGUST ▸ NOVEMBER)

CHARCOAL BURNER
RUSSULA CYANOXANTHA
(AUGUST ▸ OCTOBER)

MILKY CAP
LACTARIUS DELICIOSUS
(SEPTEMBER ▸ NOVEMBER)

YELLOWFOOT CHANTERELLE
CRATERELLUS TUBAEFORMIS
(SEPTEMBER ▸ FEBRUARY)

YELLOWFOOT CHANTERELLE
CANTHARELLUS LUTESCENS
(SEPTEMBER ▸ FEBRUARY)

WHITE TRUFFLE
TUBER MAGNATUM
(OCTOBER ▸ DECEMBER)

BLACK TRUFFLE
TUBER MELANOSPORUM
(OCTOBER ▸ MARCH)

BLEWIT
LEPISTA NUDA

HORSE MUSHROOM
AGARICUS ARVENSIS

CREMINI
AGARICUS BISPORUS

BUTTON MUSHROOM
AGARICUS BISPORUS

PORTOBELLO
AGARICUS BISPORUS

BRANCHING OYSTER MUSHROOM
PLEUROTUS CORNUCOPIAE

PEARL OYSTER MUSHROOM
PLEUROTUS OSTREATUS

KING OYSTER MUSHROOM
PLEUROTUS ERYNGII

LUNG OYSTER MUSHROOM
PLEUROTUS PULMONARIUS

SHIMEJI
HYPSIZYGUS TESSULATUS

BLACK POPLAR, PIOPPINO
AGROCYBE AEGERITA

SHIITAKE
LENTINULA EDODES

ENOKI, GOLDEN NEEDLE
FLAMMULINA VELUTIPES

BLACK MOREL
MORCHELLA CONICA

BLOND MOREL
MORCHELLA ESCULENTA

WHITE MUSHROOM
AGARICUS BISPORUS

PORCINI
BOLETUS EDULIS

SHIITAKE
LENTINULA EDODES

FAIRY RING
MARASMIUS OREADES

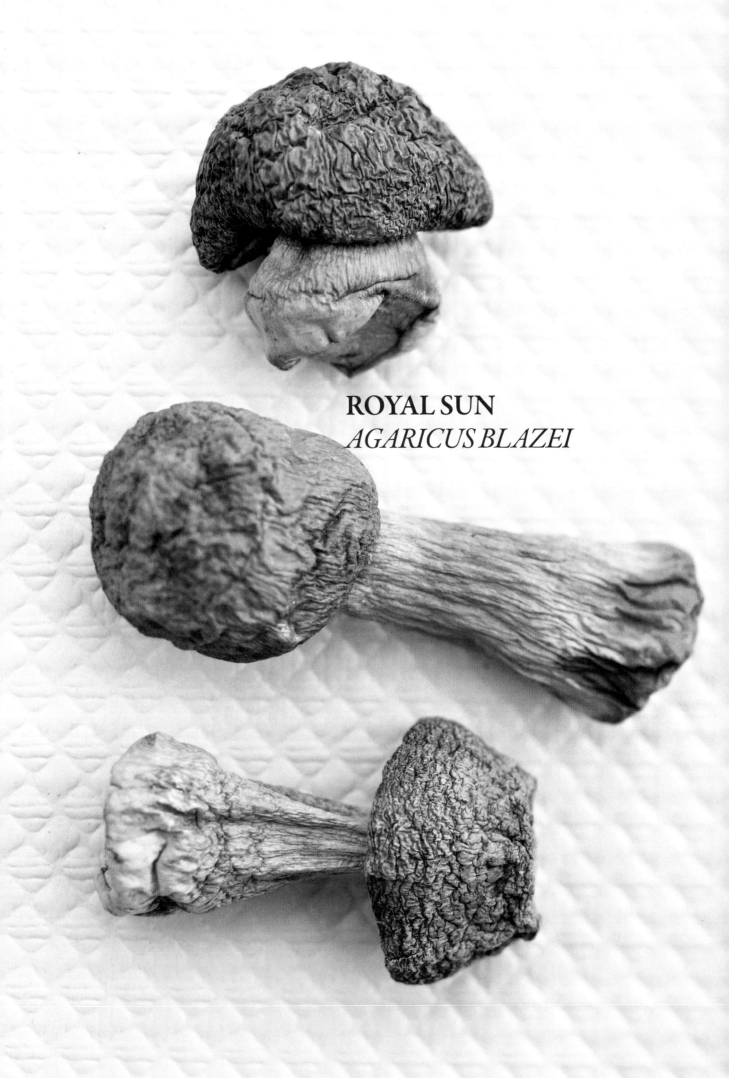

ROYAL SUN
AGARICUS BLAZEI

SHAGGY MANE
COPRINUS COMATUS

ST. GEORGE'S MUSHROOM
CALOCYBE GAMBOSA

ENOKI, GOLDEN NEEDLE
FLAMMULINA VELUTIPES

POM POM, BEAR'S HEAD
HERICIUM ERINACEUS

WOOD EAR, JUDAS EAR
AURICULARIA AURICULA-JUDAE

PARASOL MUSHROOM
MACROLEPIOTA PROCERA

REISHI
GANODERMA LUCIDUM

BLUSHING MUSHROOM
CANTHARELLUS RUBESCENS

WILD
MUSHROOMS

FRESH MORELS

This is the first mushroom to pop up after the winter lull.

You'll see morels on market shelves in most regions starting in early April, at the same time as asparagus, green garlic, and lemon verbena.

Generally quite expensive at the beginning of the season (around $50 per pound), morels become a bit more affordable later in the season, but are still a luxury ingredient, and one that's becoming increasingly rare. There are several types of morel, including the black morel and the blond morel. Either type will work perfectly in these recipes. The black makes the best dried morel, while the blond—the one you most commonly find at markets—is better fresh, and is usually larger and great for stuffing.

CHOOSE: Firm, with a clean stem, giving off a lightly musky mushroom fragrance. If it smells like a boys' locker room after a championship game, give it a pass.

CLEAN: Brush out the little crevices, trim the stem, and check the hollow cap for hitchhikers (slugs, bugs).

COOK: Morels contain a mild toxin that's thermolabile, meaning it's active in the raw state but disappears with cooking. Because of this, you should always cook morels between 10 and 15 minutes over low heat in whole butter, taking care that they don't dry out (add a little wine or stock, or cover the pan during cooking).

MORELS AND LEMON VERBENA EN PAPILLOTE

SERVES 4 / 20 MINUTES PREP TIME / 20 MINUTES COOKING TIME

7½ oz morels, cleaned
2 tablespoons butter
⅓ cup fino sherry or vin jaune
1 bunch fresh lemon verbena
A bit of olive oil
Eight 8-inch-square pieces Japanese rice paper or parchment
Salt and freshly ground black pepper

We've borrowed this papillote technique from the kitchens of Akira Oshima, chef of the restaurant Yamazato in Amsterdam. Here, we're using sherry instead of sake; the flavor of whatever wine you use is infused into the ingredients because the bamboo-based paper absorbs it nicely, yet doesn't get soggy. You can find Japanese rice paper at art supply stores.

Cook the cleaned morels in the butter over low heat for 10 minutes, along with 1 tablespoon of water. Add half the wine and 1 sprig of the lemon verbena, and then cover the pan and continue cooking for another 5 minutes.

Preheat the oven to 425°F. Lightly oil one sheet of paper (using a pastry brush). Pour the remaining wine into a shallow dish and quickly dip another piece of paper into the wine. Lay the wine-dipped sheet evenly on top of the first sheet. Repeat with the remaining paper to make four papillotes.

Divide the morels and the cooking juices among the papillotes, arranging the ingredients in a pile on one half of each square; add a fresh sprig of lemon verbena to each one and season with salt and pepper. Fold over the other half of the paper and then seal the edges by making tiny folds along the edge to crimp and seal, making a pouch. Slide the papillotes onto a baking sheet, put into the hot oven, and bake for about 5 minutes.

Remove from the oven and carefully slice or snip open the papillotes immediately before serving.

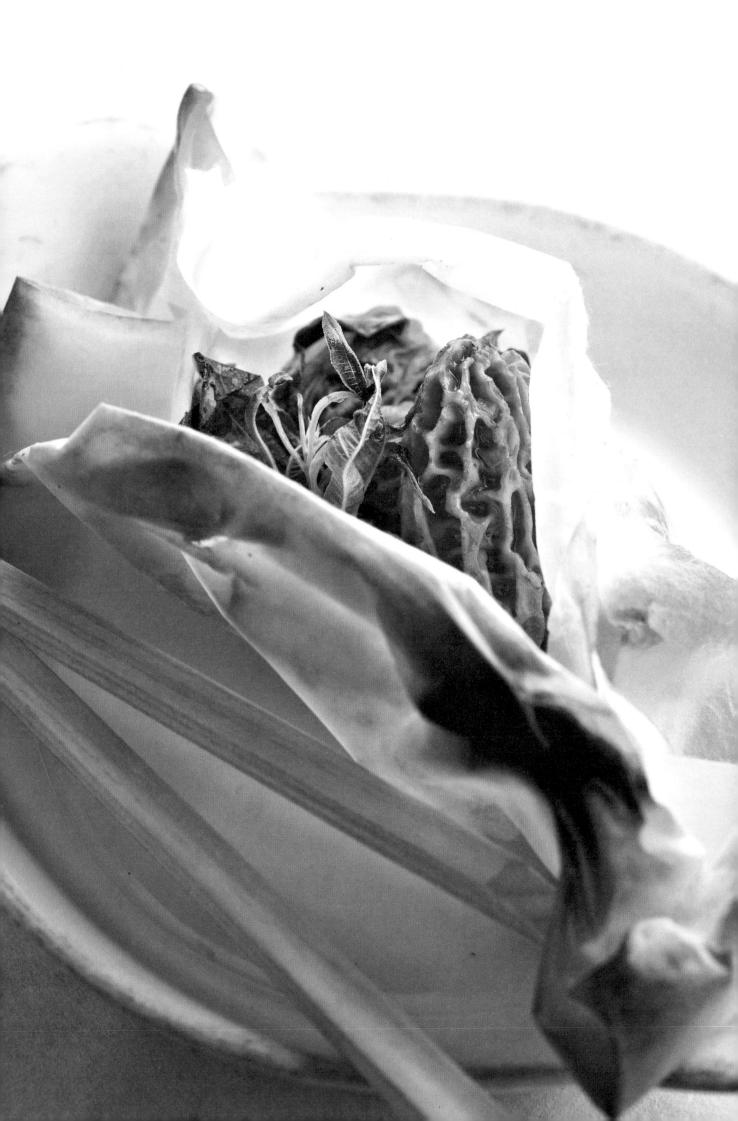

MORELS WITH SWEET WINE AND WHITE ASPARAGUS

SERVES 4 / 15 MINUTES PREP TIME / 20 MINUTES COOKING TIME

4 eggs
8 fat white asparagus spears
14 oz fresh morels, cleaned
2 tablespoons butter
⅓ cup sweet white wine, such as Sauternes, Muscat de Beaumes de Venise, or white Rivesaltes
Salt and freshly ground black pepper

Soft-boil the eggs. Lightly peel the asparagus and then boil in lightly salted water for about 5 minutes, so they're tender but still firm. Refresh them in ice water and then drain them well. Simmer the morels over low heat in the butter and wine, for 5 minutes with the pot covered, and then 5 minutes more, uncovered, over medium heat. Add the asparagus and continue cooking another 5 minutes. Add just a pinch of salt. Peel the egg. Top each portion with the egg, and season generously with the pepper before serving.

MORELS STUFFED WITH FOIE GRAS

SERVES 4 / 20 MINUTES PREP TIME / 20 MINUTES COOKING TIME

14 oz blond morels, on the large side, cleaned
1 small shallot, minced
2 garlic cloves, minced
3 tablespoons butter
1 large slice good bread, such as pain au levain
1 slice cured ham, such as prosciutto
1 sprig thyme
6 oz foie gras (goose if you can get it, but duck is lovely), cooked or *mi-cuit* (half-cooked)

Cook the morels with the shallot and garlic over low heat with the butter and 1 tablespoon of water, for about 10 minutes covered, and another 5 minutes, uncovered. Cool the morels, so they're not warm when you stuff them.

Lightly toast the bread and the slice of ham in the oven (so they both dry out a bit). Put the bread, ham, and thyme leaves into a food processor and pulse to make crumbs.

Preheat the broiler. Slip little pieces of the foie gras into each morel, arrange them in an ovenproof gratin or shallow casserole dish, sprinkle generously with the ham and bread crumbs, and then broil for about 5 minutes until heated through and nicely browned. Serve immediately.

GRATIN OF MORELS AND GREEN ASPARAGUS

SERVES 4 / 20 MINUTES PREP TIME / 25 MINUTES COOKING TIME

8 green asparagus spears
3.5 oz morels, on the small side, cleaned
1 tablespoon butter
¾ cup crème fraîche or heavy cream
1 egg yolk
1 oz grated Comté or other similar French cheese such as cave-aged Gruyère or Beaufort
Whole nutmeg
4 small sprigs savory

Peel the ends of the asparagus, then boil in lightly salted water for 2 to 4 minutes, depending on their size. They should stay crisp-tender. Refresh them in ice water and drain well. Simmer the morels over low heat in the butter with 1 tablespoon of water for about 15 minutes.

Preheat the broiler. Mix the crème fraîche, egg yolk, cheese, and a few scrapes of fresh nutmeg. Arrange the asparagus, morels, and a sprig of savory in each of four small ovenproof gratin dishes and then pour the custard on top. The asparagus shouldn't be totally covered. Slide the dishes under the broiler for 5 to 10 minutes, until the custard is just barely set and the gratins are beautifully golden. Serve immediately.

Pages 72–73: Morels Stuffed with Foie Gras; Morels with Sweet Wine and White Asparagus

ST. GEORGE'S MUSHROOMS

You'll start seeing these mushrooms in many regions around April 23—the feast of St. George. They are highly perishable and so don't travel far from where they're foraged, and very rare in the United States. Look for them at farmers' markets and greengrocers through the middle of May, and if the season isn't too dry, you might be graced with a brief comeback in June. In spite of their scarcity, the price is pretty reasonable and the quality is uniformly good. They're easy to clean, with firm dense flesh, a mildly bitter flavor, and a fragrance that brings to mind freshly ground flour.

CHOOSE: St. George's mushrooms should be firm and tightly formed, creamy or very light beige in color, parasite-free (check for bugs at the point where you trim the stem). They should have a clean, pleasant smell.

CLEAN: Sort through them to pick out any bits of grass (they grow in grassy fields and clearings). Trim a bit off the stem and give them a light brushing, if need be. Discard any stems that are housing bugs.

COOK: When they're really fresh, they're delicious raw. After a day or so, they'll begin to oxidize and the color will darken, so it's better to cook them at that point (sauté quickly in olive oil or clarified butter).

ST. GEORGE'S MUSHROOMS WITH MAYONNAISE

SERVES 4 / 5 MINUTES PREP TIME

10.5 oz St. George's mushrooms
½ cup lemony mayonnaise
Fleur de sel (or other good sea salt)
1 lemon
1 tablespoon freshly grated Parmesan cheese (optional)

Sort through the mushrooms and brush off any that aren't perfectly clean. Arrange each mushroom, cap-side down, on a little dollop of mayonnaise (just a suggestion; feel free to improvise other presentations). Sprinkle with salt and serve with lemon wedges.

Another idea is to make a lemon-salt by mixing the fleur de sel with some finely grated lemon zest (from an organic or unsprayed lemon). Sprinkle that on the mushrooms along with the Parmesan.

◀ ## ST. GEORGE'S MUSHROOM TARTARE

SERVES 4 / 10 MINUTES PREP TIME

10.5 oz St. George's mushrooms
2 tablespoons olive oil
4 tablespoons chopped pitted black olives
2 minced shallots
4 tablespoons chopped, drained capers
12 chopped cornichons
1 bunch chives, snipped
4 egg yolks
1 or 2 sprigs basil
Parmesan cheese shavings (optional)

Make this dish like you were making a steak tartare: Coarsely chop the cleaned mushrooms and mix them with the olive oil, olives, shallots, capers, cornichons, and half the chives.

Arrange on four plates with an egg yolk on each one. Top with the rest of the chives, the basil, and, if you like, the Parmesan shavings before serving.

ST. GEORGE'S MUSHROOMS SAUTÉED WITH ARTICHOKES AND PRESERVED LEMONS

SERVES 4 / 15 MINUTES PREP TIME / 15 MINUTES COOKING TIME

1 pint cherry tomatoes
8 baby artichokes, stems trimmed, leaf tips cut off
2 preserved lemons, quartered
¼ cup olive oil
Salt and freshly ground black pepper
14 oz St. George's mushrooms

Preheat the broiler. Prick each tomato with a skewer and arrange them on a baking sheet, along with the artichokes and preserved lemons. Drizzle everything with 3 tablespoons of the olive oil, season with salt and pepper, and broil just until the tomatoes burst and the artichokes are tender.

Meanwhile, clean the mushrooms, trim the stems, and sauté them quickly over medium-high heat with the rest of the olive oil.

Combine and serve hot.

Pages 78–79: St. George's Mushrooms Sautéed with Artichokes and Preserved Lemons (both photos of same dish)

FAIRY RING MUSHROOMS

Fairy rings are, in my opinion, the most delicious of the springtime mushrooms, arriving usually in April, right after morel season; they make sporadic appearances in the fall as well. The mushrooms grow in tight little groups in grassy fields, sometimes growing in a circular pattern (known also as fairy rings or pixie rings). They are easy to cook, and they make perfect partners for other springtime fare: asparagus, green garlic, spring onions, salad greens, mild fish, spring veal, and more.

CHOOSE: Fairy ring mushrooms should be dry and an even, delicate beige. Watch out, because some vendors will spray the mushrooms with water in order to pump up their weight (they're quite light to begin with), which also changes their color to a dark brown. Don't get duped.

CLEAN: The small size and somewhat floppy and sometimes ridged stem makes cleaning fairy rings frustrating. The best thing to do is simply sort through them, picking out the bits of grass and twigs leftover from foraging, and then to snip the stems of the biggest ones with some scissors. Plan on a handful per person.

COOK: Fairy rings love butter, goose fat, cream, and gentle cooking methods. When you first start cooking them, add a bit of broth, meat drippings, or wine to the pan. Their delicate and distinct fragrance of bitter almonds and hazelnuts infuses into whatever liquid you cook the mushrooms with, making fairy rings perfect for sauces, soups, or confits. The flavor is even stronger in the dried version (see Dried Fairy Ring Mushrooms, page 236).

ASPARAGUS AND ARTICHOKES
WITH BUTTERED FAIRY RING MUSHROOMS

SERVES 4 / 15 MINUTES PREP TIME / 10 MINUTES COOKING TIME

8 gorgeous fat asparagus spears
2 artichokes
1 lemon, cut into thick slices
4 eggs
14 oz fairy ring mushrooms
2 tablespoons butter

Cook the asparagus for 4 to 6 minutes in boiling salted water until crisp-tender and then refresh them in very cold water; drain. Pare the artichokes until you just have the meaty bottoms, and then steam them on some lemon slices until tender, about 15 minutes. Cut the artichoke bottoms into slices.

Boil the eggs for 5 minutes. Refresh in cold water; peel and halve them. Gently sauté the fairy ring mushrooms in the butter over low heat. Arrange everything together on plates to serve.

This recipe works beautifully with spaghetti squash, which is in season at the same time. Substitute the asparagus and artichokes with the squash. Boil or steam it about 20 minutes. Scrape out the interior with a fork and toss with a bit of butter.

VEAL CHOPS WITH FAIRY RING MUSHROOMS IN CREAM

SERVES 2 / 15 MINUTES PREP TIME/ 15 MINUTES COOKING TIME (+ 10 MINUTES RESTING)

2 veal chops, about 1½ inches thick
Salt and freshly ground black pepper
2 tablespoons clarified butter (see page 18)
⅓ cup good white wine
1 tablespoon butter
14 oz fairy ring mushrooms, stems trimmed
¾ cup crème fraîche

Season the veal chops with salt and pepper, and sauté them in the clarified butter in a nice Dutch oven or heavy skillet over medium-high heat. Take them from the pan, set aside, and keep warm. Pour off the fat from the pan. Add the wine and deglaze to dissolve the cooked-on juices. Boil until reduced to just a glaze. Add the 1 tablespoon butter, decrease the heat, and then add the fairy ring mushrooms. Cook for about 10 minutes. Add the crème fraîche, and let the mushrooms infuse into the cream over very low heat, without boiling, for a good 5 minutes more. Serve the mushrooms and the veal on warmed plates; you can keep the chops whole or cut the meat from the bones and cut it into thick slices.

BANON CHEESE WITH FAIRY RING MUSHROOMS SAUTÉED WITH WALNUTS

SERVES 4 / 15 MINUTES PREP TIME (+1 HOUR RESTING) / 2 MINUTES COOKING TIME

⅔ cup walnuts
⅓ cup sweet white wine such as Sauternes, late-harvest Riesling, or Muscat de Beaume-de-Venise
4 Banon cheeses (a fresh goat cheese wrapped in chestnut leaves), or other fresh goat cheese, about 3½ oz each
14 oz fairy ring mushrooms, stems trimmed
3 tablespoons clarified butter (see page 18)
Good-quality bread, toasted, for serving

Soak the walnuts in the wine for an hour.

Partially unwrap the cheeses and let them sit at room temperature. Sauté the fairy ring mushrooms in the clarified butter over low heat. Increase the heat to medium and add the soaked walnuts. Cook for about 2 minutes, then serve with the cheeses and bread.

NEW POTATOES SAUTÉED WITH MORELS AND FAIRY RING MUSHROOMS

SERVES 4 / 10 MINUTES PREP TIME / 25 MINUTES COOKING TIME

Perfect to accompany a roast chicken.

1 lb small potatoes, such as a fingerling variety
10½ oz morels
½ lb fairy ring mushrooms
2 tablespoons butter
⅓ cup rich chicken broth
Salt and freshly ground black pepper

Cook the potatoes for 20 minutes in salted water. Brush off the morels and trim the fairy ring stems. When the potatoes are cooked, drain them. Sauté the morels in the butter over low heat for 10 minutes. Add the fairy ring mushrooms and keep cooking for another 10 minutes, adding a little broth every few minutes. Add the potatoes and cook for another 3 minutes to marry the flavors. Season with salt and pepper, then serve.

Pages 84–85: Veal Chops with Fairy Ring Mushrooms in Cream; New Potatoes Sautéed with Morels and Fairy Ring Mushrooms

SUMMER TRUFFLES

You'll find summer truffles beginning around mid-June, mostly coming from Italy and the south of France, though other regions of the world have their own version of a local truffle. Summer truffles struggle from an identity crisis—on the one hand, they're considered a luxury ingredient, but on the other hand, they're looked down upon as being inferior to the "real" truffle, the black Périgord truffle *(Tuber melanosporum)*, which is considered more important, more delicious, and way more expensive (around four times as expensive as the summer truffle).

In other words, the summer truffle *(Tuber aestivum)* doesn't get much respect, which is a shame. It's true that the aroma of a summer truffle is subtle. The flesh, which is light in color, is delicately crunchy, with an earthy quality and a very light musky flavor that's characteristically "truffle-y." So despite the fact that summer truffles aren't as gastronomically exciting as a black truffle, don't overlook them. Their affordable price, flavor, mystique, and the fact that they are a slightly exotic, wild food means they can still add a special touch to summer meals.

CHOOSE: Look for nice round specimens; if they're too misshapen, they're hard to clean. The minimum size should be about 1 oz (about the size of a golf ball), and they should be very firm, even hard. Avoid truffles that are caked with dirt—it's a good way to preserve truffles but makes it hard to see any flaws and also makes them weigh more (and therefore cost more).

CLEAN: Brush them thoroughly (rinsing them under a stream of cool water, if they're particularly gritty). Peel them lightly with a vegetable peeler, evening out the bumpy surface. This will make them easier to slice and will minimize the "earthy" scent.

COOK: Recipes for black truffles generally are not well suited for summer truffles. While cooking brings out all the best qualities in a black truffle, it simply dampens the flavor of a summer truffle. They should always be eaten raw, either grated or thinly sliced, and always as simply as possible, with a minimum of ingredients.

TOMATO AND SUMMER TRUFFLE SALAD

SERVES 4 / 5 MINUTES PREP TIME

4 to 8 tomatoes (beefsteaks or smaller slicers)
1 small pink radish
1 small red bell or other sweet pepper
1 spring onion
Fleur de sel (or other good salt)
Freshly ground black pepper
1 large summer truffle (1½ to 2 oz), brushed clean
A few leaves of purple basil
¼ cup mild olive oil
1 to 2 tablespoons sherry or red wine vinegar

Rinse and trim the tomatoes, radish, bell pepper, and onion and slice them thinly. Season with fleur de sel and pepper. Cut the truffle into extremely thin slices. Arrange the ingredients so the salad looks pretty; decorate with the basil leaves. Season again and drizzle with the olive oil and vinegar before serving.

SALAD OF WHITE PEACH, MOZZARELLA, AND SUMMER TRUFFLE

SERVES 4 / 5 MINUTES PREP TIME

2 large white peaches, ripe but still firm
1 large summer truffle (1½ to 2 oz), brushed clean
1 large ball (or 2 smaller balls) buffalo mozzarella
¼ cup good olive oil
1 tablespoon balsamic vinegar
Salt and freshly ground black pepper
Grilled bread for serving

Cut the peaches into quarters, discarding the pit but leaving the skin on. Cut the truffle into thin slices, and cut the mozzarella into quarters. Arrange the ingredients on four salad plates and drizzle with the olive oil and a few drops of vinegar. Salt lightly and pepper generously. Serve with grilled bread to absorb the bright, luscious flavors.

AGARICS AND SUMMER TRUFFLE SALAD

SERVES 4 / 5 MINUTES PREP TIME

14 oz agarics (from the forest or fields), cleaned and trimmed
3.5 oz summer truffles, brushed clean
3 to 4 tablespoons walnut or hazelnut oil
Fleur de sel (or other good salt) and freshly ground black pepper

This salad couldn't be simpler or more elegant: just slice the mushrooms and truffles and season with oil, salt, and pepper before serving.

ROASTED NEW POTATOES WITH SUMMER TRUFFLES

SERVES 4 / 15 MINUTES PREP TIME / 20 MINUTES COOKING TIME

1 head of garlic
1 lb new or creamer (small) potatoes
2 tablespoons grapeseed oil or clarified butter (see page 18)
Fleur de sel (or other good salt)
3.5 oz summer truffles, brushed clean

Separate the garlic cloves from the head, leave them unpeeled, and precook them by steaming or boiling for about 10 minutes.

Preheat the oven to 425°F. Cut the potatoes in half, toss them with the grapeseed oil, and arrange them, cut-side down, on a buttered or oiled baking sheet. Distribute the precooked garlic cloves over the potatoes and season everything generously with fleur de sel. Cook for 10 minutes, then decrease the oven temperature to 300°F and cook up to 10 minutes more. The potatoes should be golden brown and crisp on the outside, creamy and melting on the inside.

Arrange on plates, season again with salt if need be, and shave the truffle over the potatoes before serving.

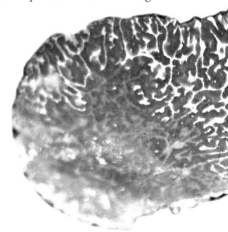

SARDINE AND SUMMER TRUFFLE TART ▶

SERVES 4 / 15 MINUTES PREP TIME / 40 MINUTES COOKING TIME

2 lb cherry tomatoes
1 head garlic, separated into cloves
1 or 2 onions, cut into chunks
5 to 6 sprigs fresh thyme
3 pinches sugar
Salt
10 oz uncooked puff pastry dough (store-bought is fine)
Two 3.75-oz tins good-quality sardines in oil, drained
3.5 oz summer truffles, brushed clean

Preheat the broiler. Spread out the tomatoes in a shallow ovenproof baking dish and prick each one with a skewer. Add the garlic, onion, and thyme; sprinkle with the sugar and 3 pinches salt and slide under the broiler. After 20 minutes, when the tomatoes have browned and collapsed a bit, remove from the heat and set aside (if the tomatoes have given off too much juice, think about pouring some off so the pastry doesn't get soggy).

Adjust the oven to 400°F. Roll out the dough to a large rectangle (about 9 by 14 inches) and transfer it to a baking sheet, or roll it out and line a removable-bottom tart pan with it. Spread the tomato compote over the dough and bake the tart for 20 minutes, or until the bottom is nicely browned. About 5 minutes before the tart is cooked, arrange the sardines over the tart. Remove the tart from the oven, top the whole thing with shaved truffle and season with salt. Serve hot.

LASAGNE OF SMOKED BUTTER AND SUMMER TRUFFLES

SERVES 4 / 20 MINUTES PREP TIME / 10 MINUTES COOKING TIME

2 tablespoons unsalted butter
½ teaspoon smoked salt
2¾ oz summer truffles, brushed clean and sliced
8 sheets fresh lasagne noodles
2 oz Parmesan cheese curls

Melt the butter with the smoked salt and add the sliced truffle. Set aside.

Cook the lasagne noodles in a large pot of salted boiling water according to package instructions, until al dente. Drain well.

In an ovenproof casserole, layer the lasagne noodles alternately with the truffle butter and top with the Parmesan. Serve right away, or reheat the lasagne for a few minutes in a 400°F and serve hot.

CHANTERELLE MUSHROOMS

The season for chanterelles starts in May, and lasts through the summer. Though highly prized and practically iconic, a chanterelle is, in my mind, just not that exciting to cook with. Small (1¼ to 2 inches), very fresh ones are best, with firm, lightly fibrous flesh. Also called girolles or golden chanterelles, their fragrance is indeed similar to a fresh apricot, and they are high in beta-carotene (vitamin A).

CHOOSE: Color is key. Look for bright yellow-orange or else creamy beige (for chanterelles from dry regions or that grow near chestnut trees). If they're dark or brownish orange, they're likely waterlogged or have been poorly handled in transit, so take a pass. If you're buying a whole flat or basket of them, be sure to inspect the ones on the bottom as well as the ones on display in the top layer.

CLEAN: When gathered from dry mossy spots, all you need to do is a quick sort and a light brushing. If the chanterelles were foraged from a wetter area, under leaf cover for example, you'll need to be more diligent in your sorting and brushing, and you may even need to rinse them and then dry them by laying the chanterelles on a clean kitchen towel in a cool spot.

COOK: Perfect young specimens can be eaten raw, and you can also simply blanch them in boiling water or some white wine. But the best method for chanterelles is sautéing, either quickly over high heat, in which case they get browned and stay slightly crunchy, or else slow-sautéing for around 15 minutes, until nicely caramelized. Anything between those two methods will just give you watery, blah chanterelles. If they do give off lots of liquid during cooking, pop them into a strainer to drain off the excess halfway through, and then put them back in the pan to finish. Chanterelles love to be finished with olive oil, goose fat, and a nice chunk of butter.

MARINATED CHANTERELLES AND APRICOTS WITH HAM

SERVES 4 / 15 MINUTES PREP TIME

14 oz very young chanterelles (dry and firm)
4 small, ripe but firm apricots, pitted and quartered
4 slices cured ham (such as prosciutto or Serrano), cut into thin strips
¼ cup mild, fruity olive or canola oil
Salt
A few leaves purple basil

Brush off the chanterelles but don't rinse them. Toss them gently with the apricots and ham strips. Drizzle with the olive oil and allow to marinate for 10 minutes. Season with salt and garnish with a few basil leaves before serving.

◀ ## GNOCCHI WITH CHANTERELLES

SERVES 4 / 20 MINUTES PREP TIME / 15 MINUTES COOKING TIME

14 oz chanterelles
2 tablespoons olive oil
4 sprigs thyme or marjoram (or a mix of the two)
14 oz gnocchi
2 oz Parmesan cheese shavings

Sauté the chanterelles in the olive oil with the herbs.

Cook the gnocchi in boiling salted water (they're done when they float to the surface). Drain well, then add them to the pan with the chanterelles. Add the Parmesan and serve right away.

DUCK CONFIT WITH CANDIED CHANTERELLES

SERVES 4 / 5 MINUTES PREP TIME/ 10 MINUTES COOKING TIME

4 duck legs
A couple dozen Candied Chanterelles (page 269)

Preheat the oven to 400°F. Put the duck legs in a shallow ovenproof baking pan and cook until they have rendered their fat and the skin is golden brown. This should take about 10 minutes. Remove from oven and rest until cooled enough to handle. Pull the meat from the bone and serve on top of the candied chanterelles.

ZUCCHINI BLOSSOM–CHANTERELLE JAM

SERVES 4 / 30 MINUTES PREP TIME / 15 MINUTES COOKING TIME

1¾ oz pine nuts
⅓ cup golden raisins
¼ cup olive oil
10½ oz small chanterelles, nice and dry
2 sprigs flat-leaf parsley
1 small, fresh hot chile, cored, seeded, and minced
10 zucchini blossoms, torn in half
Salt

Toast the pine nuts lightly in a dry skillet over medium heat. Soak the raisins in about half of the olive oil for 20 minutes. Sauté the chanterelles over medium heat in the rest of the oil until they're golden brown. Add the parsley and chile.

Simmer over low heat for 10 minutes, and then add the zucchini blossoms.

Season with salt and continue cooking over low heat another minute or so. Store in an airtight container in the refrigerator for up to 1 week.

This is delicious served warm with polenta, stuffed summer vegetables, or roast chicken.

Pages 98–99: Candied Chanterelles; Duck Confit with Candied Chanterelles

CAESAR'S MUSHROOMS

Oddly, the genus of mushrooms that includes the most deadly mushroom *(genus Amanita)* also includes one of the most delicious—the Caesar's mushroom. Their appearance is rather startling: They grow in a thick white capsule that looks like an egg (called *ovulo* in Italian), from which they hatch when mature. Once out of the "egg," they thicken up and the golden-yellow color of their gills intensifies. Their superior eating qualities are pretty much undisputed—more or less etched in history, really, having been considered a delicacy since Roman times, which is when they got their name.

CHOOSE: On the young side, clean, and with a fruity fragrance.

CLEAN: If they're still in the "egg," carefully peel it off. You can eat the mushrooms raw in a salad; they have a delicate and slightly resinous flavor, which pairs nicely with fruity, fragrant oils (such as olive and pumpkin seed). For more mature mushrooms, cut off the thickest part of the stem, and pull away the thin membrane that covers the cap.

COOK: Cut them into quarters to cook *en persillade* (sautéed with garlic and parsley), which will bring out their more assertive, fruity side.

CAESAR'S MUSHROOM SALAD
SERVES 4 / 10 MINUTES PREP TIME

10½ oz Caesar's mushrooms
4 tablespoons olive or canola oil
A few Parmesan cheese curls
Salt
¼ teaspoon fennel seeds, toasted and crushed (optional)
1 teaspoon grated lemon zest (optional)

Choose young mushrooms, if possible, still partly covered with their white coating. Remove the coating, trim the stems, and cut the caps into ½2- to ⅟₁₆-inch slices. Arrange them on plates, drizzle with the olive oil, and top with the Parmesan and a lightly sprinkling of salt. Sprinkle with the fennel and lemon zest, if you like before serving.

CAESAR'S MUSHROOMS WITH OLIVE OIL, LEMON, AND SAGE
SERVES 4 / 10 MINUTES PREP TIME / 5 MINUTES COOKING TIME

14 oz Caesar's mushrooms
1 tablespoon olive oil
Half a lemon
2 sprigs sage, cut into fine shreds
Salt

Peel the mushrooms, if needed, and cut them into quarters. Add the olive oil to a pan set over medium heat. When hot, add the mushrooms and sauté for 2 minutes. Squeeze in the lemon juice, add the sage, decrease the heat to low, and continue cooking for 2 minutes. Season lightly with salt and serve right away.

PARASOL MUSHROOMS

These mushrooms are everywhere in the woods and fields, and yet you rarely see them on market shelves. When you do find parasol mushrooms at the market, they're often in sorry shape. But you might get lucky!

CHOOSE: The caps should be beige with dark brown flecks, with slightly soft but dense flesh. They should have a pleasant smell.

CLEAN: Parasol mushrooms are always sold without their stems, which are tough. If the stems are still attached, simply pinch and twist them off.

COOK: Large specimens with very open caps can be as wide as your open hand; they are best sautéed in butter or breaded and fried. Their flavor is meaty and nutty. The smaller ones, which are firmer and more tightly closed, are best grilled or stuffed. Parasol mushrooms are very fragile and should be eaten within two or three days of picking.

BROILED PARASOL MUSHROOMS ▶

SERVES 4 / 10 MINUTES PREP TIME / 10 MINUTES COOKING TIME

14 tablespoons unsalted butter, at room temperature
1 small handful mixed fresh herbs (such as parsley, tarragon, oregano, chervil), minced
12 parasol mushroom caps, not too open
1 cup fresh bread crumbs
Salt
A splash of lemon juice

Preheat the broiler. Make an herb butter by mashing together the butter and the herbs.

Put the mushroom caps in an ovenproof dish, open-side up, and put a piece of herb butter in each cap. Sprinkle everything with the bread crumbs.

Slide the dish under the broiler. When you hear the butter start to sizzle, the dish is ready. Salt lightly, drizzle with the lemon juice, and whatever you do, don't forget some good bread. It's a sin to not sop up the sauce!

GRILLED PARASOL MUSHROOMS

SERVES 4 / 30 MINUTES PREP TIME / 5 MINUTES COOKING TIME

1 cup butter
1 bunch fragrant herbs (thyme, sage, rosemary, savory, oregano, or a mix)
12 parasol mushroom caps, quite open

Melt the butter, clarify it if you like (see page 18), and infuse it with the herbs by letting them sit together for at least 20 minutes (you can do this the night before).

Preheat an outdoor grill. When your grill is hot, dunk the mushroom caps in the melted herb butter and grill for just a few minutes on each side. Serve hot.

PAN-FRIED PARASOL MUSHROOMS

SERVES 4 / 10 MINUTES PREP TIME / 5 MINUTES COOKING TIME

1 tablespoon clarified butter (see page 18)
4 large parasol mushroom caps
1 tablespoon butter
2 tablespoons chopped fresh parsley

Heat a skillet to medium, add the clarified butter, and arrange the mushrooms in the pan in an even layer. After a few minutes, turn the mushrooms, add the whole butter, decrease the heat, and continue cooking another 2 minutes. Sprinkle with the parsley before serving.

PARASOL MUSHROOMS, CORDON BLEU–STYLE

SERVES 4 / 15 MINUTES PREP TIME / 10 MINUTES COOKING TIME

8 parasol mushroom caps, slightly open
4 thin slices Gruyère cheese
5 oz sliced, cooked ham
½ cup all-purpose flour, for dredging
1 egg, lightly beaten
1¾ cups fresh bread crumbs
1 tablespoon clarified butter (see page 18)
Salt and freshly ground black pepper
¼ cup chopped fresh parsley
1 lemon, quartered

Make four "sandwiches" by layering a mushroom cap (open-side up), a slice of cheese, a slice of ham, and another mushroom cap (rounded-side up). Squeeze gently to secure.

Carefully dredge the sandwich in the flour, then using tongs, dip into the beaten egg, and then the bread crumbs. Heat the clarified butter in a nonstick pan over medium heat and sauté the sandwiches about 5 minutes each side. Season with salt and pepper. Serve with the chopped parsley and a lemon wedge.

PARASOL MUSHROOM FRITTERS

SERVES 4 / 15 MINUTES PREP TIME / 2 MINUTES COOKING TIME

4 large parasol mushroom caps, quite open
4 cups grapeseed, peanut, or canola oil, for frying
1¼ cups flour
1 teaspoon baking soda
½ cup chilled white wine
⅓ cup ice water
1 lemon, quartered

Cut the mushroom caps in quarters. Heat the oil in a large pot to 350°F (leave plenty of head room in case the oil bubbles up). Whisk together the flour, baking soda, wine, and ice water to form a batter (don't worry if there are a few lumps). Dip the mushroom quarters into the batter. Fry a few at a time, about 2 minutes. Drain them on a clean kitchen towel or paper towels and serve with the lemon wedges.

HEDGEHOG MUSHROOMS

This mushroom has quite a bit in common with a chanterelle: it's popular and well-liked, easy to find at the market, and—unfortunately—it has pretty limited potential in the kitchen.

CHOOSE: The hedgehog's distinctive appearance may have a lot to do with its appeal. They are a creamy beige, delicate, and slightly velvety, curvy and compact, with the underside of the cap covered with tiny spines. You can't confuse them with any other mushroom variety because of their unique look.

CLEAN: Usually all you need to do is scrape off the spiny bits from under the cap, using the rounded end of a spoon or a paring knife with a curved blade.

COOK: You can eat young hedgehog mushrooms raw or just quickly sautéed (which preserves their color and texture). As they age, however, they darken and get slightly bitter. For older hedgehogs, quickly blanch them in boiling water with some lemon juice squeezed in it, and once drained and dried, you can fry them. They'll darken during cooking and give off their liquid, which you need to pour off. Cook them until they turn a nice light orange color again.

HEDGEHOG MUSHROOM REMOULADE

SERVES 4 / 10 MINUTES PREP TIME

1 lb young hedgehog mushrooms
½ cup mayonnaise
1 lemon
2 tablespoons Dijon mustard
2 tablespoons chopped capers

Clean the mushrooms, brushing away all the spines from under the caps. Cut the mushrooms into thin slices. Mix together the mayonnaise, lemon juice to taste, and mustard. Add the capers and mushrooms, and it's ready to serve.

PIG'S FEET AND HEDGEHOG BASTILLAS ▶

SERVES 4 / 25 MINUTES PREP TIME / 10 MINUTES COOKING TIME

4 pig's feet
1 lb hedgehog mushrooms
1 shallot, chopped
1 tablespoon clarified butter (see page 18)
1 bunch flat-leaf parsley, chopped
Salt and freshly ground black pepper
8 sheets brick pastry (thin Moroccan pastry, similar to filo) or filo dough
1 tablespoon olive oil

Preheat the oven to 375°F. Put the pig's feet on a baking sheet and roast until slightly browned and softened. Remove from the oven and let rest until cool enough to handle, then pull the meat from the bones.

Sauté the mushrooms and shallot in the clarified butter over medium-high heat.

Chop the boned meat and toss together with the mushrooms and parsley. Season generously with salt and pepper.

Set metal rings on a baking sheet. Arrange two sheets of the pastry in each ring, letting the excess hang over the edges. Fill with the meat and mushroom mixture, fold over the pastry to make a nice round packet. Add the olive oil to a hot skillet and cook the bastillas over medium heat until they are heated through and the pastry is nicely browned, about 5 minutes on each side. Serve hot.

You'll need four 4-inch metal rings for this preparation.

PORCINI MUSHROOMS

The porcini is a mythic mushroom. Also called a cèpe or king bolete, it's the mushroom that immediately comes to mind when you think of the bounty of the forest. The porcini is inextricably woven into so many European cuisines, especially those of the rural and mountainous regions. Unfortunately porcini are becoming scarce, especially outside of their growing areas, and their prices are bordering on obscene.

CHOOSE: Porcini should be firm and not too spongy, preferably split lengthwise so you can make sure the interior isn't bug-infested. You can also sometimes find porcini "corks," which are mini-mushrooms, that can pop up from the earth in a matter of hours. Shaped like a Champagne cork, with a sweet and chubby stem and a small cap, these mushrooms are prized, and priced accordingly. As a matter of principle, however, don't buy any porcini that are in fact smaller than a large wine cork—they are immature and should not have been picked.

CLEAN: How you clean porcini is a matter of their age, where they were picked, and their condition. Cork-size porcini haven't developed any spongy tubes yet and are rarely bug-infested, so they're a cinch to clean.

COOK: Small cork-size porcini are great for serving raw (thinly sliced), sautéed (halved), or marinated (whole). Medium porcini that are still firm are perfect for grilling, and you can even stuff the caps. The largest porcini, which are often soft and spongy, and slightly musky smelling, are best cleaned and cut up before adding to long-cooked dishes (stews and braises, or as part of a stuffing). There are a few mushroom varieties that are related to the porcini (bay bolete, summer cèpe, or bronze cèpe) which are tasty and can be cooked in the same manner.

RAW MUSHROOM SALAD

SERVES 4 / 10 MINUTES PREP TIME

4 small porcini
A few mixed fresh wild mushrooms such as agarics, creminis, summer truffles, hedgehogs, or chanterelles
¼ cup olive oil
Fleur de sel (or other good salt) and freshly ground black pepper

Clean all the mushrooms without rinsing them (a brush is a good idea).

Slice the mushrooms right before serving. Tumble them gently to mix, so they don't crumble.

Arrange the mushrooms on plates and drizzle with the olive oil. Season with fleur de sel and pepper before serving.

PORCINI AND CHESTNUT SOUP

SERVES 4 / 15 MINUTES PREP TIME (+ OVERNIGHT INFUSION) / 20 MINUTES COOKING TIME

¾ cup whole milk or cream
½ oz dried porcini
14 oz porcini, with the spongy undersides scraped out
1 tablespoon clarified butter (see page 18)
7 oz cooked chestnuts
4 cups vegetable, mushroom, or chicken broth
Salt and freshly ground black pepper

The night before, pour the milk over the dried porcini, refrigerate, and leave to infuse overnight.

The day you want to serve the soup, cut the cleaned raw porcini in pieces and sauté them in the clarified butter in a medium saucepan over medium heat for about 10 minutes. Crumble in the chestnuts, add the broth and the infused milk (discard the dried mushrooms).

Simmer over low heat for about 10 minutes. Season with salt and pepper. Blend everything in a blender and keep warm until ready to serve.

GRILLED PORCINI MARINATED WITH WHITE GRAPES

SERVES 4 / 20 MINUTES PREP TIME (+ 2 HOURS RESTING) / 10 MINUTES COOKING TIME

4 medium porcini
1 bunch white or green grapes
⅓ cup olive oil
Whole black peppercorns

Cut the porcini into thick slices (scrape out any spongy parts from under the caps). Grill the mushrooms on an oiled grill pan or broil them on an oiled baking sheet, about 10 minutes, turning once. Arrange the slices on a serving platter. Peel the grapes (or not) and distribute them over the mushrooms. Pour the olive oil over the porcini and grapes. Sprinkle with a few peppercorns.

Chill for at least 2 hours. Serve with grilled bread to absorb the earthy, fruity flavors.

PORCINI AND CHANTERELLES WITH PERSILLADE

SERVES 4 / 30 MINUTES PREP TIME / 15 MINUTES COOKING TIME

1 lb chanterelles
1 lb medium porcini
1 bunch flat-leaf parsley
1 shallot
3 garlic cloves
¼ cup clarified butter (see page 18)
1 tablespoon butter
Salt

Brush the chanterelles to clean them, sort by size, and cut the largest ones in half. Brush the porcini, and cut them into pieces.

Wash the parsley, pull off the leaves and chop them. Finely chop the shallot. Peel the garlic cloves and blanch them twice to mellow their flavor (put them in a small pot, cover with cold water, bring to a boil, drain, and repeat). Crush and mince the garlic.

In a nonstick skillet, heat the clarified butter and sauté the mushrooms over high heat for 7 to 8 minutes. When they have browned, decrease the heat to medium and add the garlic, and then half of the parsley and all of the minced shallot. Cook another 4 to 5 minutes. Add the rest of the parsley, the whole butter, and then season with salt. (Don't ever salt during cooking, or the mushrooms will give off too much liquid and won't brown properly.) Serve hot.

SAUTÉED PORCINI AND APPLES

SERVES 4 / 20 MINUTES PREP TIME / 15 MINUTES COOKING TIME

8 small porcini
2 small shallots
2 apples
2 tablespoons clarified butter (see page 18)
1 handful of fresh parsley, chopped
2 tablespoons butter
1 pinch fleur de sel (or other good salt)

Cut the porcini in half lengthwise. Mince the shallots. Peel the apples and cut them into thin wedges.

Sauté the porcini in the clarified butter over high heat for about 5 minutes. Decrease the heat, and add the shallots, apples, and half the parsley. When everything is nicely browned, add the whole butter and the rest of the parsley. Season with fleur de sel. Serve hot.

PORCINI STEW WITH COFFEE

SERVES 4 / 15 MINUTES PREP TIME / 1½ HOURS COOKING TIME

This recipe is one of the few that can be made successfully with frozen porcini.

2¼ lb porcini
¼ cup clarified butter (see page 18)
¾ cup dry white wine or sweet white wine such as Sauternes or late-harvest Riesling
1 strong shot of espresso
2 sprigs of parsley, chopped
Salt and freshly ground black pepper

Cut the porcini into pieces, scraping away any spongy undersides, if necessary. Sauté the mushrooms with the clarified butter over high heat in a Dutch oven for about 5 minutes. Add the white wine, decrease the heat, and let simmer 1 hour, covered. Uncover, add the espresso and parsley, and then continue to simmer another 15 minutes. Season with salt and pepper. Prop fingers of toasted or grilled bread alongside each serving for dipping.

If you like, after adding the espresso and parsley and seasoning with salt and pepper, you can cover the pot with puff pastry and finish cooking in a hot oven (about 425°F) for 10 to 15 minutes.

FRICASSEE OF PORCINI WITH VEAL BROTH AND BAY LEAVES

SERVES 4 / 30 MINUTES PREP TIME / 15 MINUTES COOKING TIME

8 young, firm porcini
1 tablespoon butter
4 bay leaves
1 sprig fresh thyme
1¼ cups rich veal or chicken broth

Briefly sauté the porcini in a skillet with the butter over medium heat. Transfer them to a small saucepan, add the bay leaves and thyme, and then the broth.

Simmer over medium-low heat until the liquid has reduced to a glaze (about 15 minutes), taking care to not let it cook until it's completely dry. The reduced broth should cloak the mushrooms. Serve very hot.

This rich, earthy dish is delicious spooned over a starchy accompaniment such as polenta.

Pages 112–115: Porcini and Chanterelles with Persillade; Porcini and Chestnut Soup; Sautéed Porcini and Apples; Fricassee of Porcini with Veal Broth and Bay Leaves

111

STUFFED PORCINI CAPS

SERVES 4 / 30 MINUTES PREP TIME / 15 MINUTES COOKING TIME

4 large or 8 medium porcini, with nicely shaped caps
2 tablespoons goose fat or clarified butter (see page 18)
A few chestnut leaves (optional)
1 thick slice bacon, ham, or some foie gras (or all three), chopped
1 slice stale bread, soaked in milk and squeezed
1 egg
2 sprigs parsley, coarsely chopped
Salt and freshly ground black pepper
½ cup fresh bread crumbs

Preheat the oven to 350°F. Separate the porcini stems from the caps. Sauté the caps, rounded-side down, in the goose fat over medium-high heat. Drain, arrange (preferably on a bed of chestnut leaves) in a small ovenproof baking dish, and set aside. Mince the porcini stems and sauté them (adding a little more fat if needed) for 10 minutes.

Put the sautéed stems, bacon, bread, egg, and parsley into a food processor and pulse to mix. Season with salt and pepper. Shape little balls of stuffing and fill each mushroom cap. Sprinkle the bread crumbs over the mushrooms and bake for 15 minutes. Serve hot.

BAKED EGGS AND SPELT

SERVES 4 / 20 MINUTES PREP TIME (+ 2 HOURS RESTING) / 10 MINUTES COOKING TIME

¾ cup uncooked spelt
10½ oz chopped porcini
2 tablespoons butter
1 large sprig flat-leaf parsley, chopped
1¾ cups heavy cream
3½ oz semifirm cow's or sheep's milk cheese, grated
4 eggs
Salt

Rinse the spelt and cook until it is just tender (following the instructions on the package). Sauté the porcini in the butter over medium-high heat until golden, then add the parsley and cream. Simmer for a few minutes until the cream is slightly reduced.

Divide the cooked spelt and the cheese among four ovenproof glasses or ramekins, top with the creamed porcini, and chill for 2 hours. Right before cooking, carefully break one egg into each glass and cook for 10 minutes in a steamer or in a covered Dutch oven filled with about an inch of water. Season with salt, and serve with toast points for dipping.

Pages 118–119: Porcini Stew with Coffee; Baked Eggs and Spelt

RUSSULA MUSHROOMS

This is a large family of mushrooms, only found in the wild. Some varieties are quite respectable—in particular, the charcoal-burner russula, which you may encounter at many farmers' markets in the Great Lakes region.

CHOOSE: The cap color varies from gray to greenish; the stem and gills will always be white. Once cooked, the mushrooms are very fragile; look for young ones.

CLEAN: Trim off the stem at the point where it breaks easily from the cap. The underside of the caps can sometimes appear slightly greasy, which can give the impression that the mushrooms are dirty. Use a soft brush to clean out any bits of soil stuck between the gills, but don't rinse. And know that russulas are vulnerable to larva—examine carefully.

COOK: A classic approach is best, such as *persillade*, starting by sautéing in clarified butter and finishing with some whole butter. The results are fragrant and crunchy.

RUSSULAS PERSILLADE
SERVES 4 / 10 MINUTES PREP TIME / 10 MINUTES COOKING TIME

Serve with Boar Stew (recipe follows).

1 garlic clove
1 bunch flat-leaf parsley
1 lb charcoal-burner russulas
2 tablespoons clarified butter (see page 18)
1 tablespoon butter
Salt

Blanch and chop the garlic. Rinse, dry, and chop the parsley. Brush off the mushrooms and trim their stems, keeping the caps intact. Sauté the mushrooms over high heat in the clarified butter for about 5 minutes. Decrease the heat, add the garlic and half the parsley and let cook another 5 minutes. Right before serving, add the whole butter and the rest of the parsley. Season with salt.

BOAR STEW ▶
SERVES 4 / 15 MINUTES PREP TIME / 5 HOURS COOKING TIME

1¾ lb boar, cut into 3½-oz chunks
2 tablespoons olive oil
1 large onion, chopped
2 carrots, chopped
5 garlic cloves
Bouquet garni (fresh parsley, thyme, and rosemary, tied with a leek green)
10 whole black peppercorns
3 whole juniper berries
4 cups full-bodied red wine
2 cups veal broth
1 tablespoon tomato paste
Salt and freshly ground black pepper

Brown the boar in the olive oil in a Dutch oven over medium-high heat, then pour off any excess grease. Add the onion, carrots, garlic, bouquet garni, peppercorns, juniper berries, wine, broth, and tomato paste. Season generously with salt and pepper. Simmer, covered, over low heat until the meat is very tender, 4 to 5 hours. Take out the meat and strain the rest of the ingredients through a fine sieve into a clean pot, pressing on the solids to get all the flavor. If the sauce is a bit thin, continue to simmer until it's reduced to a nice consistency. Pour the sauce over the meat and keep warm until serving.

BLACK TRUMPET MUSHROOMS

These are fragile, slightly stringy funnel-shaped mushrooms that you'll see beginning around late summer on through early winter, in abundant quantities. The color, which ranges from intense black to a bluish gray (when they're quite dry), is a function of the zinc content of the mushroom. The overall quality of the mushroom depends on where and when it was foraged. Also called trumpets of death, black trumpets gathered in summer or autumn from cooler regions will be better quality.

CHOOSE: Up until early winter, cleaning is simple—open up the mushroom, brush away any bits of dead leaf, cut off any wet or gritty stem ends. Later in the season, however, it's a different story as black trumpets are often foraged from frosty, snowy areas and get delivered wet. The soil and grit dissolves into the moisture and within a day or two, the mushrooms start to liquefy and smell disgusting. So be careful when buying; check the underneath layers of the crate or basket, never buy mushrooms that are wrapped in plastic, and know that just one soggy mushroom can quickly contaminate the whole lot.

CLEAN: Sort through them frequently, and don't hesitate to wash them in a large basin of cold water with some vinegar added; swish around for a few seconds, drain, and then blot on a kitchen towel right away, or better yet, spin dry in a salad spinner. Black trumpets are stringy, so they can handle this somewhat rough handling.

COOK: Start by cooking them over medium heat in some clarified butter, goose fat, or lard. The mushrooms will give off some liquid. Strain them and put them back into a dry skillet with a bit more fat, and keep cooking until they're crispy. The mushrooms don't need to be served immediately; you can keep them warm for a bit.

CARAMELIZED BELGIAN ENDIVE WITH BLACK TRUMPET MUSHROOMS

SERVES 4 / 15 MINUTES PREP TIME / 1 HOUR, 40 MINUTES COOKING TIME

6 heads Belgian endive
A bit of Demerara sugar
3 tablespoons butter
¾ cup white wine
2 handfuls black trumpet mushrooms
Salt and freshly ground black pepper

Preheat the oven to 200°F. Cut the endive heads in half lengthwise, place them, cut-side down, on a parchment-lined rimmed baking sheet or shallow ovenproof baking dish. Sprinkle with the sugar, dot with 2 tablespoons of the butter, and add the white wine. Bake for 1½ hours until the endive is very soft and caramelized.

While the endive is roasting, wash the black trumpet mushrooms, and sauté them in the rest of the butter over medium-high heat. Season generously with salt and pepper.

Remove the endive from the oven, divide among four dishes, and top with the sautéed mushrooms before serving.

For a variation, you can arrange the roasted endive in a gratin dish, top with a custard (see page 124), and bake at 325°F until the custard is just barely firm. Then top with the sautéed mushrooms.

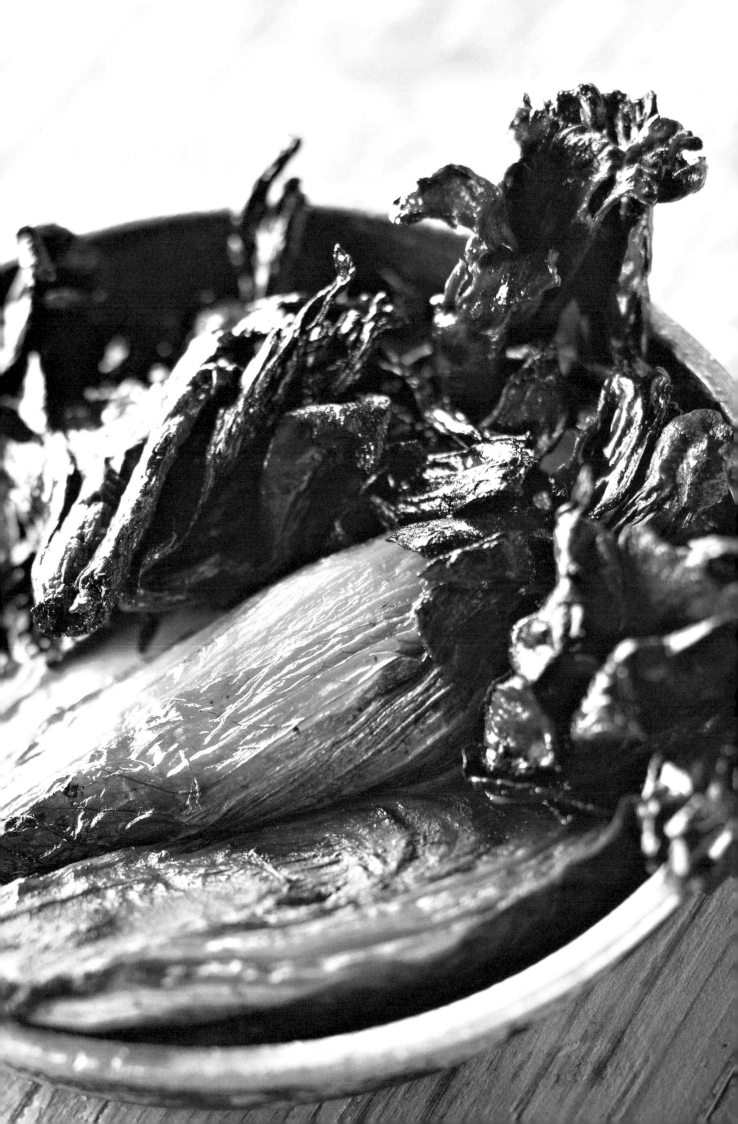

GRATIN OF ONIONS AND BLACK TRUMPET MUSHROOMS

SERVES 4 / 30 MINUTES PREP TIME / 20 MINUTES COOKING TIME

1 bunch spring onions
1 head green garlic
2 handfuls black trumpet mushrooms
2 tablespoons clarified butter (see page 18)

CUSTARD
1 whole egg
2 egg yolks
2 cups heavy cream
⅓ cup grated cheese such as Comté or Gruyère

4 sprigs of thyme
Salt

Steam the onions for about 8 minutes, and steam the garlic, unpeeled, for about 12 minutes.

Wash the mushrooms, sauté them in the clarified butter, and then keep warm.

FOR THE CUSTARD: With a fork, beat together the egg, egg yolks, cream, and cheese.

Preheat the broiler to low. Divide the onions, garlic, and thyme among four small gratin dishes. Pour the custard into the gratins. Broil for about 10 minutes.

When they are nicely browned, top with the sautéed mushrooms and season with salt before serving.

BAKED EGGS WITH BLACK TRUMPETS

SERVES 4 / 15 MINUTES PREP TIME (+ 1 TO 2 HOURS RESTING) / 10 MINUTES COOKING TIME

1 slice stale bread
1 cup grated Cantal or other firm cheese such as Gruyère
14 oz black trumpet mushrooms, cleaned
2 tablespoons butter plus 1 teaspoon
2½ cups crème fraîche
1 pinch freshly grated nutmeg
4 eggs
Salt

Arrange a piece of the bread and some of the cheese in the bottom of each of four ovenproof ramekins.

Sauté half the mushrooms over medium-high heat in 1 tablespoon of the butter, and then add the crème fraîche. Bring to a boil, boil for a few seconds, and then decrease the heat to a simmer. Add the nutmeg.

Pour the mushroom mixture into the ramekins and chill for 1 to 2 hours.

Right before serving, gently break an egg into each ramekin and either steam them for 10 minutes or cook them for 10 minutes in a covered Dutch oven to which you've added about an inch of water.

Sauté the remaining mushrooms in 1 tablespoon butter over medium-high heat, and when they are cooked, let them continue to cook over low heat with the final 1 teaspoon butter until they're crisp. Season everything lightly with salt. Distribute the crisp mushrooms among the ramekins. Toast points alongside would add a little crunch.

MILKY CAP MUSHROOMS

A fleeting pleasure, you'll only find these mushrooms on market shelves from mid-September to mid-November, and then again for one or two weeks in December, depending on whether November had any warm spells. Ideally, milky caps are crunchy and sweet, slightly resinous, sometimes reminiscent of coconuts. I say "ideally" because it's not easy to find milky caps in pristine condition, especially after mid-November, when frost and moisture can wreck them during shipping. Their stunning orange color develops verdigris discolorations, their surface becomes slightly slimy, and their smell gets strong.

CHOOSE: Look for young specimens, with caps that curl under slightly. They should be firm, bright orange (possibly with a few dark green spots), and dry.

CLEAN: In the early part of the season, milky caps are often infested with tiny insect larvae; it's best to inspect them by cutting the stem where it meets the cap.

COOK: Their characteristic resinous and slightly sour flavor means these milky caps aren't to everyone's taste, and are not too versatile in the kitchen. Except for preserved milky caps, for which you'll find variations from the Pacific Northwest to the Arctic Circle, there just aren't many recipes. For our purposes, the best way to cook these mushrooms is to grill them.

GRILLED MILKY CAPS WITH FRESH CHILE

SERVES 4 / 20 MINUTES PREP TIME / 10 MINUTES COOKING TIME

1 fresh sweet red chile, such as lipstick or cherry popper pepper
12 milky cap mushroom caps
4 tablespoons olive oil
2 slices cured ham, such prosciutto or Serrano
2 tablespoons fresh bread crumbs

Preheat the broiler. Chop the chile into little pieces and put it in a bowl with the mushrooms and olive oil. Marinate for about 10 minutes. While you're doing that, toast the ham in the oven for a few minutes to dry it out, and then pulse in a food processor with the bread crumbs. Arrange the mushrooms on a baking sheet, distribute the chiles over top, and sprinkle with the ham–bread crumb mixture. Broil for about 10 minutes, or until browned and hot through. Serve hot.

Page 127: Grilled Milky Caps with Maroilles Cheese

GRILLED MILKY CAPS WITH SAFFRON ▶

SERVES 4 / 10 MINUTES PREP TIME (+ 1 HOUR RESTING) / 10 MINUTES COOKING TIME

4 tablespoons olive oil
4 sprigs thyme (or oregano, savory, or all three)
1 pinch saffron threads
12 milky cap mushroom caps

Preheat the broiler. Mix the olive oil, herbs, and saffron together in a small bowl. Add the mushrooms and marinate for about an hour. Arrange the mushrooms on a baking sheet and broil until softened, about 10 minutes. Serve hot.

GRILLED MILKY CAPS WITH MAROILLES CHEESE

SERVES 4 / 10 MINUTES PREP TIME / 10 MINUTES COOKING TIME

12 milky cap mushroom caps
2 tablespoons gin (optional)
7½ oz Maroilles cheese with rind removed (or other washed-rind cow's milk cheese), thinly sliced
Freshly ground black pepper

Preheat the broiler. If you like, sprinkle the mushrooms with the gin and flambé them. Then arrange the mushrooms in four small ovenproof gratin dishes (or a large one). Arrange the cheese slices over the mushrooms. Broil until browned and bubbly. Season generously with pepper and serve with a slice of great bread.

MILKY CAP CHUTNEY

SERVES 4 / 15 MINUTES PREP TIME / 10 MINUTES COOKING TIME

14 oz milky cap mushrooms
1 handful dried apricots
1 slice butternut squash (optional)
2 sweet onions (such as Vidalia or Walla Walla)
2 tablespoons olive oil
2 tablespoons golden raisins
1 garlic clove, crushed
1 small fresh red chile, cored, seeded, and minced (optional)
2 tablespoons honey
⅔ cup good wine vinegar

Dice the mushrooms, apricots, squash (if using), and onions. Cook them gently over low heat in the olive oil with the raisins, garlic, and chile (if using) for about 10 minutes. Stir in the honey and vinegar.

Cook until the mixture has reduced to a nice jammy consistency, and then let cool. Store in an airtight container in the refrigerator for up to 1 week.

Dollop on foie gras toasts, roast chicken, or cold roast meat for a delicious sweet-hot counterpoint.

CAULIFLOWER MUSHROOMS

An unusual and delicious autumn mushroom, the cauliflower has been enjoyed mostly by well-connected connoisseurs, but lately it's showing up more frequently on the shelves of well-stocked gourmet markets. Its size is quite remarkable, with specimens weighing up to 15 pounds. It's shaped like a large ball, with a very short stem that branches out to form complicated lobes. The texture is very fragile and slightly cartilaginous. The whole thing is edible. The flavor is delicate and mild, and the aroma it gives off during cooking is quite bewitching, smelling of hazelnuts and the forest floor.

CHOOSE: Look for light beige color and a fairly large size, with a pleasant odor of mossy forest floor. As cauliflower mushrooms get older, they begin to shrivel and darken and the fragrance will fade.

CLEAN: This is a mushroom that grows very rapidly at the base of pine trees. As it gets bigger, it envelops all the debris that's fallen from the trees above (pine needles, leaves, etc.). The best way to approach cleaning is to break the mushroom into pieces and pick out the debris, bit by bit. If the pieces are still gritty, you can run them under cool water, and dry them carefully on a clean dish towel. If the stem, which is dense and short, is also still gritty, simply peel it with a paring knife.

COOK: You can serve it raw or steamed; the flavor is less pronounced when cooked, but it keeps its crunchy texture. If you want to sauté it, cook it quickly over high heat, preferably in butter (clarified butter, if possible). If you cook it for too long, it becomes an unappetizing dull brown.

GRATIN OF RAVIOLI AND CAULIFLOWER MUSHROOMS

SERVES 4 / 15 MINUTES PREP TIME / 10 MINUTES COOKING TIME

1 lb prepared cheese ravioli or cheese tortellini
14 oz cauliflower mushrooms, cleaned
3 tablespoons butter
1 bunch green onions, white and light green parts, chopped
1¾ cups heavy cream
2 egg yolks
1 pinch freshly grated nutmeg

Boil the pasta until just al dente; drain well. Distribute among four gratin dishes.

Coarsely crumble the mushrooms and sauté quickly over medium-high heat in 2 tablespoons of the butter. Sauté the green onions in the remaining butter. Divide the mushrooms and onions among the gratin dishes. Preheat the broiler.

Whisk together the cream, egg yolks, and nutmeg. Pour the custard over the ravioli and mushrooms and broil for about 10 minutes, or until golden brown. Serve hot.

STEAMED CAULIFLOWER MUSHROOM AND NAPA CABBAGE

SERVES 4 / 10 MINUTES PREP TIME / 8 MINUTES COOKING TIME

Simple, straightforward, and delicious!

1 large cauliflower mushroom (1 to 1½ lb)
1 small, loose-leafed cabbage, such as Napa
Freshly ground black pepper
4 tablespoons salted butter

Trim the base of the mushroom and cut it into four thick slices; clean well. Cut the cabbage into four crosswise slices. Put the cabbage slices in a steamer basket, place the mushroom slices on top, and steam for 7 to 8 minutes. Transfer to small bowls, season each with pepper and 1 tablespoon butter, which will melt into the warm dish. Serve immediately.

YELLOWFOOT CHANTERELLE MUSHROOMS

You'll find several species of this family of mushrooms beginning in the fall and staying plentiful until winter, all throughout Europe and North America. Ranging in color from gray to yellow to orange, yellowfoots grow in great patches that, for ease of harvest, are often gathered with a rake rather than by hand (a practice that is detrimental both to the quality of the mushrooms and for the mushroom foraging beds).

As with all mushrooms gathered late in the year, early-season yellowfoot chanterelles, harvested in dry weather, are tastier than late-season ones, when everything's a bit wetter.

Though their colors are different, they have the same shape—thin, with slightly stringy flesh that forms a hollow tube topped by a funnel-shaped crown. Their fragrance is different, however—more fruity and delicate for the yellow, more musky and earthy for the gray.

CHOOSE: Favor the younger, drier specimens. Their color and smell should be clean. And choose yellowfoot chanterelles with stems that are cut or torn, a sign that they've been gathered by hand.

CLEAN: These mushrooms grow in moss, which can get into the crevices or on the stem, so get rid of it. Their funnel shape is a perfect receptacle for vegetal debris as well as insects, especially with a grayish cousin to the yellowfoot chanterelles, which are called "tubular." Tear open larger mushrooms to inspect the interior, and brush away anything unwanted.

COOK: Start cooking mushrooms over medium heat in olive oil or over higher heat in clarified butter. At first, unless they're super-dry, the mushrooms will render a lot of liquid—this mushroom juice is delicious, you need to decide whether to pour it off and use it elsewhere or to let it evaporate and be reabsorbed by the mushrooms as they continue to cook. You can also form a flavorful emulsion by whisking the liquid with a few tablespoons of cold butter. Yellowfoots don't lose their texture when cooked in liquid, either, so they are perfect for sauce-based dishes, such as soups and sautés.

SAUTÉED SCALLOP CORAL WITH YELLOWFOOT CHANTERELLES

SERVES 4 / 15 MINUTES PREP TIME / 10 MINUTES COOKING TIME

12 scallop roe sacs ("coral")
10½ oz small yellowfoot chanterelles (choose dry ones)
1 tablespoon clarified butter (see page 18)
Salt and freshly ground black pepper
1 teaspoon red pepper purée

Rinse the scallop roe well. Sauté the chanterelles in the clarified butter over medium-high heat for about 5 minutes. If they render a lot of water, continue cooking over medium heat until it's evaporated, and then add the roe and continue cooking another 5 minutes.

Increase the heat back to medium-high and sauté another 4 minutes or so. Season lightly with salt and pepper, and serve with the red pepper purée on the side.

YELLOWFOOT CHANTERELLE LASAGNE ▶

SERVES 4 / 1 HOUR PREP TIME / 50 MINUTES COOKING TIME

2 garlic cloves
1 onion
2 tablespoons olive oil
2 bay leaves
3 large tomatoes, diced
½ lb fresh mild Italian sausage
12 oz yellowfoot chanterelles
⅔ cup white wine
1¼ cups grated pecorino cheese
12 oz fresh lasagne noodles, cooked until al dente

Peel and smash the garlic cloves, mince the onion, and cook gently over very low heat with 1 tablespoon of the olive oil for about 5 minutes. Then add the bay leaves and tomatoes and simmer for 20 minutes.

Meanwhile, remove the casings from the sausages and coarsely chop the meat.

Preheat the oven to 400°F.

In a Dutch oven, gently cook the chanterelles in 1 tablespoon olive oil over low heat; once they've given off some liquid, pour it off and reserve the liquid.

Add the sausage and wine to the chanterelles and cook until the wine has reduced. Then add the tomato sauce and 1 cup of the pecorino. Continue cooking over low heat for another 20 minutes.

Arrange alternating layers of lasagna noodles and tomato-chanterelle sauce in an ovenproof baking dish. Finish with a layer of pasta, pour the reserved chanterelle liquid over the top, and sprinkle with the remaining cheese. Bake for about 10 minutes, or until heated through and the cheese has browned. Serve hot.

PIG'S FEET STUFFED WITH YELLOWFOOT CHANTERELLES

SERVES 4 / 25 MINUTES PREP TIME / 15 MINUTES COOKING TIME

12 oz yellowfoot chanterelles
3 tablespoons clarified butter (see page 18)
1 bunch flat-leaf parsley, stems trimmed, leaves chopped
Julienned zest from 2 lemons
4 cooked pig's feet
4 squares caul fat (from your butcher)
Salt and freshly ground black pepper

Sauté the chanterelles in 2 tablespoons of the clarified butter over medium-high heat for about 10 minutes, and then add the chopped parsley leaves. Blanch the lemon zest in boiling water for a few seconds, drain well, and add to the mushroom mixture.

Remove the bones from the pig's feet, keeping the meat intact. Spread each one open on a square of the caul fat. Arrange the mushroom-lemon-parsley mixture in a line down the center of each pig's foot, season well with salt and pepper, and fold to close, wrapping the caul fat around to form a neat, tight packet.

Brown the packets in a skillet in the remaining 1 tablespoon clarified butter over medium heat, starting with skin-side down, and serve hot.

YELLOWFOOT CHANTERELLES WITH TRIPE

SERVES 4 / 20 MINUTES PREP TIME / 10 MINUTES COOKING TIME

One 28-oz jar cooked tripe (in tomato sauce, as in à la mode de Caen; can be found in specialty shops)
1 lb yellowfoot chanterelles

Put the tripe and chanterelles in a Dutch oven. Cook together, covered, over low heat for about 20 minutes, then uncovered for another 10 minutes (the idea is to infuse the sauce with the chanterelle flavor). Serve hot.

YELLOWFOOT CHANTERELLES WITH BOTTARGA

SERVES 4 / 20 MINUTES PREP TIME / 10 MINUTES COOKING TIME

12 oz yellowfoot chanterelles
3 tablespoons olive oil
2 oz bottarga, grated (can be found in specialty stores)
1 lemon, cut into wedges

Sort and carefully clean the chanterelles, splitting open the large ones and brushing off any debris.

Sauté them in half of the olive oil until they've given off some liquid and it has all been cooked off.

Finish by drizzling with the rest of the olive oil, and sprinkle with the bottarga. Serve with lemon wedges.

Bottarga is mullet roe that has been salted, sun-dried, and then coated in wax as a preservative. It's used most often in Sardinian cuisine.

CLAMS WITH YELLOWFOOT CHANTERELLES AND SAKE

SERVES 4 / 30 MINUTES PREP TIME / 10 MINUTES COOKING TIME

2¼ lb small clams (such as Manila clams)
1 lb yellowfoot chanterelles
2 tablespoons butter
¾ cup sake
4 sprigs flat-leaf parsley, chopped

Wash the clams by scrubbing them lightly together in a basin of water; rinse well.

Pick through and clean the chanterelles carefully. Cut the large ones open and brush away any debris.

In a Dutch oven, brown the mushrooms in the butter over medium heat. Add the sake and clams, cover the pan, increase the heat to high, and cook, shaking the pan, until the clams open. Sprinkle with the chopped parsley. Serve hot.

OUTDOOR
SPORES

ON MONDAY AFTERNOONS IN BRUSSELS, MUSHROOMS TAKE TO THE STREETS, AT THE PLACE VAN MEENEN OUTDOOR MARKET, ANYWAY. MUSHROOM DISHES ARE ENJOYED STREET FOOD–STYLE, SERVED STRAIGHT FROM THE SKILLET OR AS SNACKS TO BE EATEN, HOT FROM THE FIRE, AS FINGER FOOD.

HOT DOGS WITH SUMMER TRUFFLES

MAKES 8 HOT DOGS / 5 MINUTES PREP TIME / 5 MINUTES COOKING TIME

8 good-quality hot dogs
8 hot dog buns or other soft rolls
3 tablespoons tartufata (see page 259)
3 tablespoons grainy mustard
1 small summer truffle (about 1 oz), brushed clean

Boil or steam the hot dogs for about 5 minutes. Split open the buns and spread with a teaspoon of the tartufata and a teaspoon of mustard. Tuck a hot dog in each bun and grate or slice some truffle on top before serving.

TRUFFLE CROQUE-MONSIEUR

MAKES 8 SANDWICHES / 15 MINUTES PREP TIME / 4 MINUTES COOKING TIME

16 slices white sandwich bread
½ cup tartufata (see page 259)
8 slices Comté or Gruyère cheese
8 small slices cooked ham
1 black truffle (about 2 oz), brushed clean

Preheat the broiler. Spread 8 slices of bread with the tartufata, and then top each with a slice of cheese and a slice of ham. Arrange an even layer of truffle slices on the ham, and then top with a second piece of bread. Broil each side of the sandwich for about 2 minutes, until toasted and the cheese melts. Serve hot.

SAINT-FÉLICIEN AND PORTOBELLO MUSHROOM SANDWICHES

MAKES 4 SANDWICHES / 10 MINUTES PREP TIME / 5 MINUTES COOKING TIME

2 portobello mushroom caps
2 tablespoons butter
4 good quality rolls, such as ciabatta or sourdough
1 round Saint-Félicien cheese or similar small, runny, washed-rind cow's milk cheese (such as Saint-Marcellin)

Cut the portobellos in wide strips and sauté them in the butter in a skillet over medium heat for about 5 minutes. Split the rolls and evenly divide the cheese and mushroom strips between them. Serve hot.

MUSHROOM FRITTERS

10 MINUTES PREP TIME (+1 HOUR RESTING TIME) / 2 MINUTES COOKING TIME

Mixed fresh wild mushrooms (agarics, bluefoots, oyster mushrooms)
All-purpose flour, for dusting
1 egg, beaten well with a fork
Fresh bread crumbs or dried panko
Oil, for frying
Chopped fresh flat-leaf parsley
Lemon wedges
Salt

Trim the mushroom stems as needed, and cut the larger mushrooms in half. Dredge the mushrooms in the flour, and then dunk them in the beaten egg. Roll them in the bread crumbs and then arrange on a rack. Chill until ready to fry.

Heat the oil in a large pot (leaving plenty of head room so the oil doesn't bubble over) until it reaches 350°F. Immerse a few mushrooms in the oil and fry until nicely browned and heated through. Drain on paper towels or a clean kitchen towel and continue with the rest of the mushrooms. Serve with the chopped parsley, lemon wedges, and salt.

Pages 152–157: Mushroom Fritters; Hot Dogs with Summer Truffles; Truffle Croque-Monsieur; Saint-Félicien and Portobello Sandwich; Mushroom Fritters

CULTIVATED
MUSHROOMS

MUSHROOM CULTIVATION

Here's the definition of mushroom cultivation, as written in the comprehensive dictionary *Les champignons et les termes de mycologie,* by Jean Guillot, et al.: "The totality of care given to certain mushrooms in order to stimulate and encourage their growth with the goal of harvesting the product."

Seems a bit simplistic, if you think about the fact that mushrooms are the products of complex networks of mostly invisible, randomly growing underground fibers (mycelium) of which the mushroom fruit is simply the fleshy edible part.

Today you can buy mycelium for many varieties of mushroom, either as inoculated logs, as fertilized grains, or as compressed mushroom spawn. But the conditions and "totality of care" required to actually get mushrooms to grow are challenging and not really in the realm of amateurs.

The common white mushroom is the first one to have been cultivated in the West on a large, semi-industrial scale. It began in the eighteenth century outside of Paris, in caves and quarries dug into the surrounding limestone, and in proximity to the national stud farm, ahem, mushrooms thrive on composted horse manure. This is why in French, the common white mushroom is called *champignon de Paris.*

But mushroom cultivation goes back farther than the common white mushroom of Paris. In Europe, common mushrooms were grown on poplar logs as far back as the earliest centuries A.D. In Asia, species such as shiitake have been cultivated for centuries using vegetable refuse (rice chaff or trimmings from the vineyard or corn fields). Today, we're able to cultivate a considerably wider range of species. Starting with the same idea that earlier generations had of creating a renewable resource from one that grows randomly and fleetingly in nature, mushroom growers have domesticated many varieties that otherwise are becoming rare or threatened in the wild, taking advantage of new understanding of ecosystems and symbiotic relationships among plants. In particular, the truffle, which is being grown on a commercial scale, is identical to wild-harvested ones.

For the most part, the types of mushroom varieties that will be cultivated, either industrially or artisanally, will depend on market forces. That's the case with the enoki, for example. More and more people are valuing its contributions in the kitchen—in the traditional cuisines of China, Japan, and Korea, as well as Provence and other Western cuisines—in part because they are a wonderful source of umami, also known as the fifth flavor (see Shiitake Mushrooms, page 195).

gleba (black flesh), which contains
the spores (white veins)

CROSS SECTION
OF A
BLACK
TRUFFLE

peridium,
covered with tiny
cone-shaped warts

THE BLACK TRUFFLE EXCEPTION

Both the symbol of the idyllic rural lifestyle and of the rarified upper reaches of haute cuisine, this underground mushroom is a perennial topic of culinary debate.

"Underground," meaning that the fruit of the mycelium, that hard little black ball, covered with little bumps endearingly called "warts," grows under the ground (at 2 to 4 inches deep), and concentrates its spores inside. The truffle has neither stem nor cap and is not visible with the naked eye, which is why it has developed such an unstoppable system for assuring its longevity (the spreading of its spores): a potent and delicious fragrance.

If you ask an Italian which truffle is best, he'll say the white truffle. If you ask the same question of a Frenchman, he'll say the black truffle. Don't bother trying to change their minds, and in a way, they're both right. The *magnatum* (white) offers finesse and aromatic delicacy, while the *melanosporum* (black) offers rusticity, intensity, and voluptuousness.

Ethereal fragrance versus earthy sensuality, to each his own. As far as truffles from China, Morocco or Australia go—to the pigs!

One of the compounds in black truffle that makes it irresistible to the animals—pigs, dogs, goats—and men alike is testosterase, similar to testosterone, a substance that is also an aromatic compound found in sperm, which is another reason why this mushroom has such a unique, heady, compelling, and earthy character.

BLACK TRUFFLES

The truffle has become rare in France (a few dozen tons per year compared to a few hundred tons a century ago) and, since 2008, the demand has outstripped the supply. In fact, imports to truffle-loving countries have grown, and we're seeing the development of "truffle orchards" springing up in spaces unused by farms and vineyards full of trees whose roots have been inoculated by truffle mycorrhiza. But the hope of making up for the lack of wild truffles with cultivated ones remains thin. The traditional producing countries are France, Italy, Spain, and Hungary. Some limited production has been seen in Austria, Serbia, and England and in unlikely places, such as Canada, or exotic places like Australia and New Zealand.

Truffles are expensive, more than $1,600 per pound, depending on variety and abundance. In the United States, the most expensive varieties are imported from Europe. In season, summer and black truffles from Oregon can cost less than $300 per pound. In Belgium and France, Christmastime is the traditional time to lavish truffles on friends and family, and this is when the prices go way, way up.

But let's keep things in perspective: unless you're using the formula of mathematician Robert Deltheil (who makes an omelet by measuring one egg, one truffle, one egg, one truffle . . .), the amount of truffle that you need per person for most dishes is around ½ oz. In other words, a maximum of $20 per person (and that's if you splurge on truffles at Christmas!). Otherwise, do your truffle eating in November, or better still, buy them in January, February, or March. That's the time in the season when they are the ripest and most aromatic.

CHOOSE: So how to buy a truffle? First of all, know that there is no such thing as a step-right-up-have-I-got-a-deal-for-you-madame—that doesn't exist and you'll just get ripped off if you're just looking for a deal. Buy only from vendors you know and trust. Buy a truffle that smells really good. Don't buy truffles that are too small (the ideal size is between 2 and 3⅓ oz).

The truffles should be clean, and ideally without blemishes, nicks, or holes. Buy your truffles no more than a week before you're going to eat them, which will mean they're about a dozen days from harvest, which is plenty. Store them in a jar with some eggs; the eggs will absorb any excess moisture and will also absorb the truffle's perfume.

CLEAN: Use a stiff vegetable brush to remove any grit or dirt. Try not to rinse them. If you must peel your truffles, save the peelings and infuse them into a broth or mix them with butter to make truffle butter.

COOK: Eat your truffles raw or cook them very quickly in butter.

◀ ## BAKED EGGS WITH TRUFFLES
SERVES 4 / 10 MINUTES PREP TIME (+ 2 HOURS RESTING TIME) / 10 MINUTES COOKING TIME

1 black truffle
2 cups plus 2 tablespoons heavy cream
2 tablespoons tartufata (see page 259)
5 slices artisan bread
1 wedge of Brie, Chaource, or other bloomy-rind, double- or triple-cream cheese
4 eggs (that you've stored in a jar with the truffle)
Fleur de sel (or other good salt)

Peel the truffle. Chop the peelings and mix them into the cream and tartufata. In a saucepan, bring the cream mixture to a boil, and then remove from the heat. Rip one slice of bread into pieces and divide it among four ovenproof ramekins or chunky glasses; do the same with the cheese. Pour the cream into the ramekins and chill for 2 hours.

Right before serving, carefully crack each egg, letting the white fall into a ramekin, but reserving the unbroken yolks in another bowl. Steam the ramekins for about 10 minutes in a steamer or a covered Dutch oven with about an inch of water. Remove the ramekins from the steamer or pot, and top with a raw yolk, some grated truffle, and a dusting of fleur de sel. Serve with the other slices of bread.

GARLIC CONFIT AND BUTTERED TRUFFLES
SERVES 4 / 15 MINUTES PREP TIME / 10 MINUTES COOKING TIME

1 small black truffle (1 to 2 oz)
1½ tablespoons clarified butter (see page 18)
1 large head very fresh garlic
2 tablespoons butter
1 pinch granulated sugar
Fleur de sel (or other good salt)

Peel the truffle, chop the peelings, and stir them into the clarified butter. Warm the butter in a small pan over low heat. Meanwhile, separate the garlic cloves from the head, but don't peel them. Put the cloves in another small saucepan, cover with water, and bring to a simmer over medium-low heat with the whole butter and sugar. Simmer until the garlic is tender. Cut the truffle into ¹⁄₁₆-inch slices and let them soak in the clarified butter for a couple of minutes. Peel the garlic cloves, crush them, and arrange the garlic confit in little mounds on each plate. Top the garlic with a few slices of truffle and then gloss with a bit more clarified truffle butter and sprinkle lightly with fleur de sel before serving.

SASHIMI WITH LEMON AND TRUFFLE
SERVES 4 / 15 MINUTES PREP TIME

1 small black truffle (1 to 2 oz)
2 sea scallops, tough tab of muscle removed
½ lemon
12 slices very fresh raw fish (such as sea bass, sea bream, snapper)
2 tablespoons olive oil
Fleur de sel (or other good salt)

Cut the truffle into thin slices. Cut the scallops into thin slices. Peel the lemon, reserving the peel for another use; cut the flesh into very thin slices. Alternate slices of fish, scallop, lemon, and truffle. Drizzle with olive oil and sprinkle with fleur de sel before serving.

Pages 170–171: Garlic Confit and Buttered Truffles; Sashimi with Lemon and Truffle

◄ ## MACARONI AND TRUFFLE GRATIN

SERVES 4 / 15 MINUTES PREP TIME (+ OVERNIGHT INFUSION) /
15 MINUTES COOKING TIME

1 black truffle (1½ to 2 oz)
2 cups milk
1 tablespoon butter
1 tablespoon all-purpose flour
2 tablespoons grated Parmesan cheese
2 cups dried macaroni or other tubular pasta

Peel the truffle. Put the peelings in the milk and leave to infuse in the refrigerator overnight.

Strain the truffle bits from the milk and discard. Warm the milk. In a medium saucepan, melt the butter over low heat and add the flour. Blend with a wooden spoon. Then, off the heat, add the warm infused milk, stirring nonstop. Return the pan to low heat and continue cooking and stirring until the sauce has thickened, about 10 minutes. Stir in the Parmesan and grate in about half of the truffle.

Preheat the broiler. Cook the macaroni in boiling salted water until it's al dente, then drain. Divide the cooked macaroni among four individual gratin dishes, cover with the truffled béchamel, and slide under the broiler; broil until the gratins are nicely golden brown. Thinly slice the remaining half of the truffle and scatter over the gratins. Serve hot.

FENNEL CONFIT WITH TRUFFLE

SERVES 4 / 15 MINUTES PREP TIME / 45 MINUTES COOKING TIME

2 fennel bulbs
½ oz black truffle
4 cups rich chicken broth
2 tablespoons butter

Trim off any fennel fronds and stalks so that you just have two neat bulbs. Trim away any tough or damaged surface layers. Cut the bulbs in half, widthwise. Blanch the fennel for 10 minutes in boiling salted water; drain well.

Peel the truffle and cut into very thin slices. Tuck the slices between the layers of fennel. Arrange the fennel halves cut-side up in a small Dutch oven or heavy-based pan. Pour the chicken broth over the fennel, bring to a simmer, and simmer gently for about 45 minutes. Baste the fennel with the broth as it reduces and concentrates. When the fennel halves are meltingly tender, take them out, whisk the butter into the reduced broth, and spoon the sauce over the fennel. Serve right away.

Page 174: Fennel Confit with Truffle

GRILLED LEEKS WITH TRUFFLED VINAIGRETTE

SERVES 4 / 10 MINUTES PREP TIME / 10 MINUTES COOKING TIME

A dozen small leeks or slender spring onions
8 tablespoons walnut, hazelnut, grapeseed, or canola oil (or a mix)
4 tablespoons red wine or sherry vinegar
Fleur de sel (or other good salt)
Freshly ground black pepper
1 small black truffle, finely chopped (1 to 2 oz)

Trim the roots and dark green tops from the leeks and wash them well, if necessary. Make the vinaigrette by whisking together the oil and vinegar, season with fleur de sel and pepper, and whisk in the truffle. Serve together, with more fleur de sel on the side.

TRUFFLED BRIE ▶

SERVES 4 / 10 MINUTES PREP TIME (+ 24 HOURS RESTING TIME)

14-oz piece of ripe Brie
1 black truffle (2½ to 3 oz), sliced thin

Split the Brie widthwise, so you have two thinner disks. Arrange the truffle slices on the interior side of one disk, lay the other disk on top to make a sandwich. Wrap the cheese tightly in plastic wrap or a clean kitchen towel and then put it in an airtight container. Wait 24 hours before digging in, then spread on some good bread, and have fleur de sel (or other good salt) on the side.

OSSO BUCO WITH TRUFFLES

SERVES 4 / 40 MINUTES PREP TIME / 5 HOURS COOKING TIME

1 black truffle (2½ to 3 oz)
4 veal shanks, cut osso buco style (1½-inches thick)
2 tablespoons clarified butter (see page 18)
¾ cup dry white wine
1 tablespoon olive oil
2 carrots, sliced into rounds
2 leeks, trimmed, washed, and chopped
1 large onion, sliced
4 garlic cloves, smashed
1 tablespoon tomato paste
4 veal or beef marrow bones
1 bouquet garni (fresh parsley, thyme, rosemary, wrapped up in a leek green)
10 peppercorns
2 cups veal stock
4 celery stalks

Brush and peel the truffle, saving the peelings; slice the truffle and reserve. Brown the veal shanks in the clarified butter in a skillet over medium-high heat. Take the veal from the pan, add the wine, and stir to dissolve the browned cooking juices. Set aside.

Heat the olive oil in a large Dutch oven over medium heat, add the carrots, leeks, onion, and garlic and cook until soft and lightly browned, about 10 minutes. Add the veal shanks, tomato paste, marrow bones, truffle peelings, bouquet garni, and peppercorns. Add the veal stock and let everything simmer over low heat for about 5 hours. When the veal is very tender, serve it with the marrow bones, some cooking liquid, and top with sliced celery and truffle.

You can also serve the marrow bones separately, with some reduced sauce and some chopped truffle.

WHITE MUSHROOMS

So here we're talking about the mushroom with the widest audience and broadest appeal, in the United States anyway, cultivated on an industrial scale in Western Europe, North America, and beyond. But we're also talking about the mushroom that has made millions of kids hate mushrooms because they are too often poorly cooked, soggy, and slimy. We need a do-over! The white mushroom grown artisanally and in its perfect form—called "quarry blond," which is really just beige—is without a doubt one of the most delicious mushrooms. It's chewy, fruity, and fragrant. All it takes it a little bit of attention.

CHOOSE: White mushrooms come in a few different forms—tiny button mushrooms, about the size of a marble, with tightly closed caps; larger white mushrooms; cremini, which are slightly larger and darker; and portobellos, the size of your hand, which is the fully mature form of this mushroom, with a fully opened cap.

CLEAN: Cleaning is straightforward. Trim the stems by cutting off any dried or gritty ends, and lightly wipe the caps with a clean kitchen towel to remove any little bits of growing medium or dirt. Whatever you do, don't wash them.

COOK: The weak point is—as well as their reputation for blandness—their tendency to render a lot of liquid during cooking, which can make them flabby, pale, and tasteless. To cook them successfully, you can use one of two methods. First, quarter the mushrooms, which will allow them to take up less space in the frying pan than sliced mushrooms, meaning the liquid will evaporate more quickly. Start cooking at high temperature in clarified butter or goose fat. Another possible method is to start cooking the mushroom quarters "dry," with no fat of any kind, until they "whistle," which signals that steam is starting to escape. At that point, you can add the fat. Persillade (parsley and garlic) is the perfect accompaniment.

CREMINI MUSHROOMS WITH LEMON

SERVES 4 / 10 MINUTES PREP TIME (+ 15 MINUTES RESTING TIME)

14 oz very fresh cremini mushrooms
2 lemons
2 tablespoons olive oil
Salt and freshly ground black pepper

Slice the mushrooms. Squeeze the lemon juice over them and let marinate for 15 minutes. Drizzle with the olive oil and season with salt and pepper before serving.

BROILED HERB-STUFFED CREMINI

SERVES 4 / 15 MINUTES PREP TIME

8 tablespoons butter, at room temperature
1 handful mixed fresh herbs (parsley, chervil, tarragon, sage, etc.), chopped
24 cremini mushrooms
Fresh bread crumbs

Preheat the broiler. Thoroughly combine the butter and the herbs.

Snap off the mushroom stems and reserve them for another use (for example, a soup).

Fill the mushroom caps with the herb butter, arrange on a baking sheet, sprinkle with the bread crumbs, and broil for around 10 minutes, until golden brown. Serve hot; all that's needed is some great bread to sop up the butter.

"GRAND-MÈRE" SAUCE

SERVES 4 / 20 MINUTES PREP TIME / 25 MINUTES COOKING TIME

1 cup pearl onions
8 oz diced slab bacon or pancetta
1 pinch sugar
2 tablespoons butter
7 oz button mushrooms
½ cup dry white wine
½ cup chicken broth

Blanch the onions in boiling water for 1 minute; drain well. Do the same with the bacon and set aside.

Peel the onions and cut larger ones in half. Put the onions in a heavy saucepan, cover with water, add the sugar, and simmer over medium-low heat until the water is completely evaporated and the onions are lightly glazed. Add the butter, increase the heat to medium-high, and add the mushrooms and bacon. Cook, stirring, until the mushrooms are nicely browned.

Add about half the wine, let it cook almost dry, add the rest, and cook down to dry again. Continue adding and reducing the chicken broth until your ingredients are nicely cloaked in sauce. Use as a delicious sauce for light meats, or spoon into a puff pastry shell and bake.

BAKED EGGS AND MUSHROOMS

SERVES 4 / 10 MINUTES PREP TIME (+ 1 HOUR RESTING TIME) / 10 MINUTES COOKING TIME

14 oz white mushrooms
2 tablespoons clarified butter (see page 18)
1¾ cups crème fraîche
1 tablespoon Dijon mustard
1 handful ramps (or tarragon), chopped
2 slices good bread (stale or fresh), cut into small dice
3⅓ oz Emmenthal or Comté cheese, cut into small dice
4 eggs
Salt and freshly ground black pepper

Quarter the mushrooms and sauté them over medium-high heat in the clarified butter. When they're nicely browned, add the crème fraîche, mustard, and ramps and bring to a boil for a few seconds to thicken slightly.

Fill four ramekins or small ovenproof glasses with the bread and cheese, and pour the mushroom cream on top. Let rest in the fridge for about an hour or so while the bread absorbs the cream. Once the filling is set, separate the eggs and slide an egg white into each ramekin. Steam in a steamer (or a covered pot with a half-inch of water in the bottom) until set, about 10 minutes. Slip a raw egg yolk on top, season with salt and pepper, and serve with toast points for dipping.

Pages 184–185: Baked Eggs and Mushrooms; Cremini Persillade

OYSTER MUSHROOMS

This family of mushrooms, which grows in tufts on tree trunks, has become quite rare in the wild, but the commercial cultivation is quite large and developed. They grow on blocks of composted sawdust, each block made up of different components according to which variety of mushroom is growing on it. Here are the five varieties of oyster mushroom you're likely to find at the store. The choose, clean, and cook information is particular to each variety listed below.

Branching Oyster: This is one of the most common of the oyster family, with a tasty yet delicate flavor. The mass-produced specimens are watery and bland, not worth eating, but those grown with artisanal methods, on composted sawdust medium, can be delicious.

King Oyster: In the wild, these mushrooms grow in the sandy soils along some coastlines, often at the foot of the sea holly thistle. Increasingly rare in its natural habitat, king oyster mushrooms are being cultivated on straw with some success. They look similar to the branching oyster, quite compact, with a velvety brown-to-beige color. The stems are more slender and sometimes slightly offset, and quite fragile. Don't wash them; every part is edible. The flavor is quite mild and slightly meaty.

Lung Oyster: Also sometimes called Indian oyster mushroom; this variety is often confused with the king, even though they don't look anything alike. This type has a white club-shaped stem that's oversized in relation to the tiny brown cap. The texture is firm, dense and springy, and the flavor has a hint of iodine. Wrapping these mushrooms in plastic packaging, as is often the case in supermarkets, can make their flavor unpleasant.

Pearl Oyster: These are also quite common; they are a darker grayish color, with thicker flesh that needs slightly longer cooking, as though you're doing a mushroom *persillade*.

Shimeji: This mushroom *(Hypsizygus tessulatus)* is actually just a relative of the other oyster-type mushrooms, and though it's a cousin, it is quite a bit different from them both in flavor, which is slightly iodine-y and tart. These are cultivated on a mass scale in Asia and they are beginning to be cultivated in other parts of the world, usually in small-scale and sometimes organic operations. They are easy to cook and don't need any cleaning.

OYSTER MUSHROOMS WITH SEAWEED BUTTER

SERVES 4 / 5 MINUTES PREP TIME / 8 MINUTES COOKING TIME

14 oz oyster mushrooms
2 tablespoons clarified butter (see page 18)
Salt
3 tablespoons seaweed butter (prepared, or make it yourself by blending rehydrated dried seaweed with butter and a bit of salt)

Cut the mushrooms into wide strips and sauté them in the clarified butter over medium-high heat until nicely browned, 7 to 8 minutes.

Season generously with salt and serve with a pat of the seaweed butter on top.

OYSTER MUSHROOMS WITH SCALLOP KEBABS

SERVES 4 / 15 MINUTES PREP TIME / 20 MINUTES COOKING TIME

2 garlic cloves, peeled
14 oz small oyster mushrooms
3 tablespoons clarified butter (see page 18)
⅔ cup white wine
1 bunch flat-leaf parsley, chopped
12 sea scallops (with their roe, if still attached)
2 tablespoons butter
Salt

Blanch the garlic by putting it in a small saucepan, covering with cold water, and bringing to a boil. Drain and repeat, and then mince the garlic and set aside. Sauté the mushrooms over medium-high heat in 2 tablespoons of the clarified butter for about 5 minutes. Add the garlic, wine, and half the parsley; decrease the heat to medium-low; and continue cooking for another 10 minutes.

Meanwhile, skewer the scallops through their centers to make kebabs. Brown them in the remaining clarified butter, and then toss in the whole butter. When the mushrooms have finished cooking, add the rest of the parsley. Season everything lightly with salt, and serve the mushrooms with the scallop kebabs.

OYSTER MUSHROOMS SAUTÉED WITH SEA LETTUCE

SERVES 4 / 10 MINUTES PREP TIME / 15 MINUTES COOKING TIME

The seaweed gives this dish a distinctive flavor, but if you like, you can use regular tender greens, such as Bibb lettuce.

4 large oyster mushrooms, cut into thick slices
2 tablespoons butter
1 handful of dried sea lettuce (also called laver), soaked to remove salt and rehydrate

Brown both sides of the mushroom slices in the butter over medium heat.

Wrap each slice with a leaf of sea lettuce and warm slightly in the skillet. Serve warm.

SAUTÉED SQUID AND OYSTER MUSHROOMS WITH BLACK PEPPER

SERVES 4 / 5 MINUTES PREP TIME / 8 MINUTES COOKING TIME

7 oz cleaned squid (not the tentacles) cut into bite-size pieces
10½ oz oyster mushrooms
1 tablespoon clarified butter (see page 18)
Freshly ground black pepper

Score the inside face of the squid pieces in a small crosshatch pattern (to keep them from curling in the heat).

Cut the mushrooms into pieces that are the same size as the squid pieces. Sauté over medium-high heat in the clarified butter, but don't let anything brown too much. Season generously with pepper before serving.

STEAMED OYSTERS WITH SHIMEJI MUSHROOMS

MAKES 1 DOZEN OYSTERS / 20 MINUTES PREP TIME / 5 MINUTES COOKING TIME

12 oysters
2 tablespoons butter
About 7 oz shimeji mushrooms
Freshly ground black pepper

Shuck the oysters and pour off the brine.

In a large skillet, heat the butter and sauté the mushrooms over medium heat for a few minutes. Add the oysters to the pan, cover, and heat for 3 minutes. Uncover, and pile the shimeji on top of the oysters. Season with pepper before serving. (If you like, you can pile everything back into the cleaned oyster shells, for serving.)

Pages 192–193: Oyster Mushrooms Sautéed with Sea Lettuce; Sautéed Squid and Oyster Mushrooms with Black Pepper

SHIITAKE MUSHROOMS

This rustic mushroom has thick, dense flesh and is a pretty chocolate-brown color that some-times looks almost like it's flocked with white. In Japan and China, where it originated, you can still find shiitakes in the wild, growing in clusters on the stumps of a certain type of oak tree—the *shii*—but the vast majority of shiitakes on the market are cultivated. Traditionally, shiitake cultivation is performed by inoculating wooden plugs with mycelium, which are then inserted into oak logs and left outdoors. An industrial shortcut uses plastic bags filled with com-pacted sawdust, which is soaked after each round of growing.

The distinctive flavor of the shiitake comes from umami or "meatiness." Sometimes called the "fifth flavor," this concept was born in Japan in the 1980s (in Japanese, *umami* translates closer to "savoriness") and was first recognized in kombu, a seaweed that's used to make the iconic broth dashi, and subsequently in beef, cheese, asparagus, ham, shellfish, and certain mushrooms, such as shiitake or oyster mushrooms. The flavor is produced from natural amino acids released by certain proteins, perceived in the mouth by specific receptors, which seems to be an evolution-ary development born of a need to find protein-rich foods.

CHOOSE: Fortunately, it's easy to tell right away whether a shiitake has had the chance to grow in the light with dignity—in other words, artisanally vs. industrially—it will be plump, firm but supple to the touch, and an even brown with just a touch of flocking. Shiitake cultivation is fairly developed in Europe, and the demand for shiitakes is due in part to an interest in the purported pharmaceutical properties of the mushroom: "glucans, benzaldehydes, all with anti-cancer properties. Lentinan promotes the development of interleukin as well as an anti-tumor substance" (according to work done by S. Arinaga et al., published in 1992). Vitamin D and mannitol have also been found in shiitakes. Beyond its anti-tumor properties, the mushroom "stimulates the immune system and aids in managing diabetes and high blood pressure" (accord-ing to *La Mycothérapie*, A. Tardif, 2007).

CLEAN: Trim off and discard the stem, which is very fibrous, or if you'd like to use it, grate or finely chop it.

COOK: Shiitakes are fairly easy to cook. Leave the cap whole or slice it, sauté it in oil or butter, adding other liquids or not—it will stay firm and tasty.

ROASTED SHIITAKES WITH CRISP-SKINNED DUCK BREAST

SERVES 4 / 10 MINUTES PREP TIME / 20 MINUTES COOKING TIME

12 large shiitakes
1 bunch red or white spring onions
4 tablespoons olive oil
20 whole juniper berries
4 maigrets of duck (boneless moulard duck breasts)

Preheat the oven to 425°F (if you have the option, adjust the oven so the heat comes mostly from the bottom element). Cut off and discard the shiitake stems and arrange the caps on a parchment-lined baking sheet. Trim the onions, leaving ½ inch of greens, and arrange them on the baking sheet with the shiitakes. Drizzle everything with the olive oil, scatter the juniper berries on top, and roast for about 20 minutes, until the shiitakes and onions are tender and slightly collapsed and browned.

Meanwhile, score the fat side of the duck breasts in a small crosshatch pattern. Sauté them, fat-side down, for 10 minutes over high heat. Flip, decrease the heat to medium, and continue cooking for another 5 minutes. Transfer to a plate, keep warm, and let rest for 5 minutes. Remove the mushrooms from the oven and serve with the duck breasts.

SHIITAKES WITH PLUMS

SERVES 4 / 10 MINUTES PREP TIME / 20 MINUTES COOKING TIME

12 shiitakes
1 tablespoon clarified butter (see page 18)
8 small firm but ripe plums, such as Damson or Italian prune plum
2 tablespoons butter
½ a fresh hot red chile, cored, seeded, and minced
Salt and freshly ground black pepper

Trim and discard the shiitake stems. Sauté the whole caps, underside down, in the clarified butter over high heat. When nicely browned, flip and continue cooking over low heat.

Meanwhile, pit the plums, cut them into wedges, and simmer in the whole butter with the minced chile until soft and compote-like. Spoon the plum compote next to the shiitakes and season generously with salt and pepper before serving.

STUFFED AND GLAZED SHIITAKES

SERVES 4 / 20 MINUTES PREP TIME (+ OVERNIGHT RESTING TIME) / 15 MINUTES COOKING TIME

12 oz mixed ground pork and veal
2 sprigs cilantro, chopped
1 small chunk fresh ginger, minced
20 medium shiitakes
2 tablespoons clarified butter (see page 18)
4 tablespoons mirin (sweet rice wine)
4 tablespoons soy sauce
4 pinches dried bonito flakes, for garnish

The night before cooking, mix together the ground meat, cilantro, and ginger. Spread in a thin layer on a plate, and leave to dry in the fridge.

The next day, cut off and discard the shiitake stems. Roll the meat mixture into 20 little balls and press firmly into the cupped side of each shiitake cap. Sauté the mushrooms, meat-side down, in the clarified butter over medium-high heat.

When the shiitakes are nicely browned, flip and add the mirin and soy sauce. Keep cooking and flipping until the liquid has reduced. When nicely glazed (7 to 8 minutes), serve on warm plates and garnish with the bonito flakes.

SUSHI BALLS ▶

MAKES 12 PIECES / 20 MINUTES PREP TIME / 10 MINUTES COOKING TIME

12 smallish shiitakes
2 tablespoons butter
1 tablespoon honey
2 tablespoons white wine
1 tablespoon soy sauce
1⅓ cups cooked and seasoned sushi rice

Trim off and discard the shiitake stems. Sauté the caps in the butter for 2 minutes, and then add the honey, wine, and soy sauce. Decrease the heat and simmer until reduced to a syrup. When the shiitakes are tender and saturated with the sauce, arrange each on a small square of plastic wrap. Roll little balls of sushi rice, top each mushroom with a rice ball, gather the plastic tightly around the mushroom and rice, and twist until they form a nice tight ball. Unwrap and serve.

Pages 198–199: Shiitakes with Plums; Stuffed and Glazed Shiitakes

BLUEFOOT MUSHROOMS

This cultivated mushroom resembles its wild counterpart, which is called the blewit, though it's less deeply colored.

CHOOSE: Bluefoot cultivation has grown in the last few years, but it's still less profitable than many other cultivated varieties. The price is nonetheless much higher than most.

CLEAN: The foot of the stem is stringy and sometimes dirty (with clinging bits of compost) and should be cut off and discarded, even on young mushrooms. With older, drier mushrooms, cut off the entire stem and cook the caps whole. You can then clean the stems and use them in another dish, chopped to add to a stuffing, or added to a broth or stock.

COOK: You can eat cultivated bluefoot mushrooms raw, though the wild ones need to be blanched before consuming. The flavor intensifies when cooked, at once sweet and musky, all the while maintaining its crisp texture. You can sauté them quickly in clarified butter, confit them in goose fat, roast them, or grill them.

BLUEFOOT MUSHROOMS WITH GARLIC AND PARSLEY
SERVES 4 / 15 MINUTES PREP TIME / 10 MINUTES COOKING TIME

2 garlic cloves, peeled
1 tablespoon goose fat, duck fat, or olive oil
About 2 dozen bluefoot mushroom caps
1 bunch fresh flat-leaf parsley, chopped
Salt and freshly ground black pepper

Blanch the garlic by bringing it to a boil in a small pan of water, draining, and repeating. Chop the blanched garlic. Heat the fat over medium heat, and then sauté the mushrooms, ribbed-sides down, for 5 minutes. Flip and add the garlic and half the parsley. Continue cooking a few more minutes and then finish with the rest of the parsley. Season generously with salt and pepper before serving.

BLUEFOOT MUSHROOMS WITH SNAILS ▶
SERVES 4 / 10 MINUES PREP TIME / 8 MINUTES COOKING TIME

About 1 dozen bluefoot mushrooms
2 tablespoons clarified butter (see page 18)
About 2 dozen cooked snails
1 tablespoon butter
2 sprigs flat-leaf parsley, chopped
1 sprig tarragon, chopped
1 handful ramps, chopped

Trim the ends of the mushroom stems and then quarter the mushrooms.

Brown them in the clarified butter over medium-high heat for 5 minutes, and then add the snails, the whole butter, parsley, tarragon, and ramps. Decrease the heat to low and cook gently for 3 to 4 minutes. Serve hot.

Page 202: Bluefoot Mushrooms with Garlic and Parsley

HORSE MUSHROOMS

Not yet well-known, horse mushrooms occasionally show up at markets throughout the United States. The wild version is pretty much extinct, thanks to pollution, but the cultivated ones—while a bit tricky to grow—are beginning to flourish.

CHOOSE: This mushroom has nothing but positives. It's beautiful, creamy white, and elegant (which earns it the nickname "snowball"); compact in shape; and very aromatic. Its characteristic fragrance is fruity and pleasantly anise-scented, and the flavor is lightly sweet (especially the stem).

CLEAN: Brush them very gently and cut the stems off if they are dry or stringy.

COOK: Horse mushrooms are easy to cook and the best recipes are those that share their organoleptic (sense-stimulating) qualities (including fennel, tarragon, etc.), and that suit the freshness level of the mushrooms. Serve raw when completely fresh, white, and crisp, and cooked once they begin to darken a bit.

HORSE MUSHROOMS WITH GARLIC AND TARRAGON

SERVES 4 / 10 MINUTES PREP TIME / 5 MINUTES COOKING TIME

1 garlic clove
1 tablespoon goose fat, duck fat, or olive oil
2 handfuls horse mushrooms
1 bunch tarragon, chopped
Salt

Blanch the garlic by bringing it to a boil in a small pan of water, draining, and repeating. Chop the blanched garlic. Heat the fat, add the mushrooms, and then sauté over high heat, stirring frequently. After about 2 minutes, add the chopped garlic and tarragon. Season with salt and serve right away.

◀ ## HORSE MUSHROOM CRISPS

MAKES 4 SMALL CRISPS / 20 MINUTES PREP TIME / 15 MINUTES COOKING TIME

CRISP TOPPING
¾ cup all-purpose flour
8 tablespoons butter
½ cup grated Parmesan cheese
⅓ cup pine nuts, lightly chopped
1 tablespoon olive oil

FILLING
12 yellow cherry tomatoes
1 tablespoon olive oil
1 pinch sugar
20 horse mushrooms, halved
1 pinch aniseed
Salt

FOR THE TOPPING: With your fingers, mix together the flour, butter, Parmesan, pine nuts, and olive oil to make a crumbly streusel. Chill until ready to use.

FOR THE FILLING: Preheat the broiler. Sauté the tomatoes in the olive oil over medium-high heat with the sugar. Add the halved mushrooms, season with the aniseed and some salt, and cook a few more minutes.

Divide the filling among four small ovenproof gratin dishes or wide ramekins, sprinkle with the crisp topping, and broil until nicely browned. Serve hot.

BLACK POPLAR MUSHROOMS

In the past, you could find this mushroom easily in the south of France, called *pivoulade*, and sold in regional markets. It grows in compact clusters (about the size of your outspread hand) on poplar logs and composted sawdust.

CHOOSE: Due to a fluctuating harvest, the price can be quite high, but the eating qualities are indisputable and worth every cent. The flesh is firm and crisp, reminiscent of walnuts.

CLEAN: Cut the base of the stem where all the mushrooms are joined and brush them off (lightly, otherwise they will darken).

COOK: You really need to cook these by simmering them in liquid. Traditionally, they would be cooked with garlic and cream, not a bad way to prepare them. For the recipes here, you can blanch the mushrooms for 1 or 2 minutes before sautéing them.

BLACK POPLAR MUSHROOMS WITH CLEMENTINES

SERVES 4 / 10 MINUTES PREP TIME / 8 MINUTES COOKING TIME

2 handfuls black poplar mushrooms
2 tablespoons clarified butter (see page 18)
2 clementines, satsumas, or small tangerines
2 tablespoons butter
Salt and freshly ground black pepper

Trim the ends of the mushroom stems. Sauté the mushrooms in the clarified butter in a skillet over medium-high heat for 4 minutes, until starting to brown. Cut the clementines in half and squeeze the juice into the skillet, reduce for a minute, add the butter, and season with the salt and pepper. Serve hot.

PERSILLADE OF BLACK POPLAR MUSHROOMS AND MONKFISH WITH MISO

SERVES 4 / 20 MINUTES PREP TIME (+ 6 HOURS RESTING TIME) / 7 MINUTES COOKING TIME

4 monkfish fillets (about 1 lb)
1 cup red miso
1 garlic clove
14 oz black poplar mushrooms
2 tablespoons clarified butter (see page 18)
2 sprigs flat-leaf parsley
Salt and freshly ground black pepper

Six hours before cooking, coat the monkfish fillets with the miso, and keep in the fridge, tightly wrapped.

Just before cooking, rinse the miso from the monkfish under cool running water. (If the fillets are a slightly scary orange color, that's a good sign!) Blanch the garlic by bringing it to a boil in a small pan of water, draining, and repeating. Chop the blanched garlic.

Sauté the mushrooms in 1 tablespoon of the clarified butter in a skillet over medium-high heat for 6 minutes, add the parsley and chopped garlic, and season with salt and pepper. Cut the monkfish fillets into very thin slices, sauté them in the remaining 1 tablespoon clarified butter for 30 seconds (they'll turn translucent white), and serve with the sautéed mushrooms.

Page 208: Persillade of Black Poplar Mushrooms and Monkfish with Miso

ENOKI MUSHROOMS

This common mushroom, which grows in the wild in dense bouquets on old logs, does very well under cultivation, where it's called enoki. You'll often see enoki mushrooms in classic Japanese dishes. The cultivated form, which is tall and white, doesn't look much like the original mushroom, and the flavor is a bit milder. The whiteness is because it's grown in complete darkness.

CHOOSE: In Asian markets (Thai, Chinese, or Japanese), you can often find enokis sold by the cluster, each weighing around 3½ oz.

CLEAN: Enokis are a cinch to prepare, just cut off the base of the cluster.

COOK: Serve them raw or cooked, simply seasoned or in a broth.

ENOKIS IN OYSTER SAUCE
SERVES 4 / 10 MINUTES PREP TIME / 2 MINUTES COOKING TIME

4 bunches enoki mushrooms
1 tablespoon grapeseed oil
4 tablespoons oyster sauce
4 tablespoons sake or mirin
2 tablespoons soy sauce
2 tablespoons fresh lime juice or yuzu juice
1 lime or yuzu, quartered, for accompaniment

Trim the base of the mushrooms, heat the grapeseed oil over medium-high, and sauté the mushrooms for about 1 minute. Gradually add the oyster sauce, sake, soy sauce, and lime juice. Reduce heat to medium and simmer until the liquid is reduced and syrupy. Serve very hot with a lime wedge or yuzu wedge.

ENOKI TEMPURA
SERVES 4 / 10 MINUTES PREP TIME / 2 MINUTES COOKING TIME

4 bunches enoki mushrooms
4 cups grapeseed oil, for frying
2 egg yolks
1¾ cups ice water
¾ cup tempura batter mix, plus more for dusting
1 large handful mixed fresh herbs (such as tarragon, chervil, cilantro), chopped
Salt
Sauce of your choice (soy sauce or mirin, for example)

Trim the base of the enokis and divide the bunches into two. Heat the grapeseed oil in a large pan (allowing plenty of room for the oil to foam up) to between 325 to 350°F. Right before cooking, whisk the egg yolks with the ice water and three-fourths of the tempura mix (sifted, if possible). Lightly flour the enoki clusters in the extra tempura flour, dunk them in the tempura batter, and fry in the hot oil for 2 minutes.

Serve with the chopped herbs, salt, and your chosen sauce.

DRIED
MUSHROOMS

DRYING

Dried mushrooms are an excellent replacement when fresh mushrooms are not available. At the very least, they also allow you to prepare specific recipes, notably infusions that can't be done with fresh mushrooms. They are indispensable in the pantry.

You can try to dry the mushrooms yourself, but the results, especially in cities, are quite random. The different techniques range from lining a crate with newspaper and letting them shrivel to stringing them on threads that resemble necklaces. Mushrooms can be dehydrated in the sun, by applying a hair dryer, or in a dehydrator. Or, you can simply buy them at the grocery store.

Currently there are relatively few commercial dried wild mushroom varieties. You see dried porcini and morels, and very few varieties of dried cultivated mushrooms. That could change, given the difficulties of supplying fresh wild mushrooms. But it is unlikely to, as harvesting areas are farther away from places of consumption, and prices continue to rise, partly because of transportation costs. The quality of these products is variable.

Mushrooms destined for drying from the beginning will be more beautiful and light, clean and clear after drying. Excellent dried mushrooms are prime specimens, dried when just-picked, as well as cleaned and cut, by hand if necessary, and dried very slowly in the oven. Sun-drying is too brutal and affects the color. The dehydrator results in a nice product, but a low yield (it's ideal for domestic use).

The price of dried mushrooms is considerably higher than that of the same mushroom when fresh for the obvious reason that it weighs 15 to 20 percent less after it has been dried.

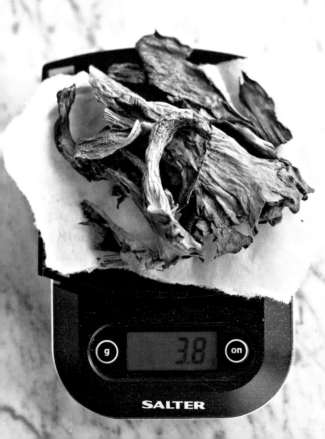

MUSHROOM RISOTTO

SERVES 4 / 30 MINUTES PREP TIME / 30 MINUTES COOKING TIME

1 onion, chopped
2 tablespoons olive oil
1¾ cup rice (Arborio or Carnaroli)
1 garlic clove, minced
7 oz dried mushrooms (one variety or a mix)
1 cup white wine
6 cups warm chicken broth or hot water
8 tablespoons very cold butter
1 bunch flat-leaf parsley
1 cup grated Parmesan cheese

Gently cook the onion in the olive oil until it's soft and fragrant, and then add the rice. Continue cooking a few minutes until the rice is glossy. Add the garlic, mushrooms, and white wine and simmer over medium heat until the wine has been absorbed. Add the broth a little at a time until the rice is nicely al dente, stirring occasionally to prevent sticking and to develop a nice starchy consistency. Finish the risotto with the butter, a ladleful of warm broth, the parsley, and the Parmesan, stirring vigorously to emulsify the ingredients and make a lovely creamy sauce. (This finishing technique is called *mantecare* in Italian.) Serve hot.

If there's any leftover risotto, reheat it in the oven topped with some buttered breadcrumbs, or shape it into balls (called arancini) *and reheat them in a skillet.*

Pages 220–223: Mushroom Risotto

DRIED PORCINI MUSHROOMS

Dried porcini, also called dried cèpes, include many varieties of this mushroom, from the most rustic to the most delicate. Much of the dried porcini production comes from Italy, though the mushrooms are usually foraged in eastern Europe and only dried and processed in Italy. The quality can be spotty, depending on the quality of the mushrooms themselves, of course, but also on the skill in drying (the best dried porcinis we've ever tasted came from Chez Fotis, in Grevena in northern Greece). The price, on the other hand, is always high. But to put things in perspective: when you dry a mushroom, it loses about 80 percent of its fresh weight, some of which is recaptured when you rehydrate it for use. Per person, you'll need only about ¾ oz dried porcini.

CHOOSE: Look for mushrooms that are an even light beige, nice flat slices, not too many bug holes, and not dusty. The fragrance is subtle, concentrated, and slightly sweet. Because of the sweet flavor and lightly chocolate-y scent, dried porcini can be used in desserts, too.

REHYDRATE AND COOK: It's easy to use dried porcini. Rehydrate them in warm water for a half hour, and then squeeze out the excess liquid. Use them as is, raw in salads, or cooked in butter or oil, with cream or not. You can also rehydrate them in milk, for a night or two in the fridge, giving you a pretty, golden-brown, porcini-flavored milk to use in any recipe calling for milk. If you've got really perfect specimens, you can eat them simply as they are, or rehydrate them directly in the skillet with butter or a bit of liquid (wine or broth).

OPEN-FACE GOAT CHEESE, PORCINI, AND SHRIMP SANDWICHES

MAKES 4 SANDWICHES / 5 MINUTES PREP TIME (+ 20 MINUTES SOAKING TIME)

1½ oz dried porcini
½ lb small deveined, cooked, and shelled shrimp
½ bunch flat-leaf parsley, chopped
4 slices good artisan bread (such as pain au levain)
1 small fresh goat cheese or sheep's milk cheese
Freshly ground black pepper
Porcini salt (see page 259), fleur de sel, or other good salt

Soak the porcini in warm water for 20 minutes. Squeeze out the water, chop the mushrooms coarsely, and mix them with the shrimp and chopped parsley.

Lightly grill the bread. Spread the slices with a generous layer of the cheese, season with pepper, and then top with the mushroom-shrimp mixture. Sprinkle with salt before serving.

PORCINI-STUFFED CABBAGE ROLLS

SERVES 4 / 25 MINUTES PREP TIME (+ 20 MINUTES SOAKING TIME) / 1 HOUR COOKING TIME

8 supple leaves Savoy cabbage
1½ oz dried porcini slices
1 slice stale bread
½ lb cooked pork or veal roast (with some leftover cooking juices, if possible)
2 slices cooked ham
1 egg
1 egg yolk
Salt and freshly ground black pepper
½ bunch parsley, coarsely chopped
2 tablespoons butter

Cook the cabbage leaves in boiling salted water until tender, and then chill in ice water to stop the cooking. Drain well.

Soak the porcini in warm water for 20 minutes; when they're soft, squeeze out excess water and chop them coarsely. Moisten the stale bread with some of the porcini soaking water to soften it a bit, and squeeze out any excess moisture from the bread.

Put the roasted meat, ham, moistened bread, whole egg, egg yolk, some salt and pepper, and the parsley into a food processor and pulse to blend. Transfer to a bowl and stir in the porcini.

Preheat the oven to 350°F. Overlap two cabbage leaves to make a nice packet, put a quarter of the stuffing in the center, and fold the leaves up to make a tight packet. Repeat with the remaining leaves and filling.

Put the cabbage rolls in an ovenproof baking dish or Dutch oven, dot with the butter, and add a tablespoon or two of water. Cover tightly and bake for about 1 hour, basting with pan juices from time to time. Serve hot.

◄ ## PIG'S EAR AND PORCINI SALAD

SERVES 4 / 15 MINUTES PREP TIME (+ 20 MINUTES SOAKING TIME)

2 cooked pig's ears
3 oz dried porcini
2 tablespoons walnut or hazelnut oil
2 tablespoons good vinegar (wine or cider vinegar)
Salt and freshly ground black pepper

Chill the pig's ears, and cut them into thin strips. Soak the porcini in warm water for about 20 minutes until soft, squeeze out the excess water, and mix them with the pig's-ear strips. Add the oil and vinegar, season with salt and pepper, and serve.

This dish is inspired by an excellent first course from the Verre Volé in Paris.

FOIE GRAS–STUFFED QUAIL WITH PORCINI SAUCE

SERVES 4 / 10 MINUTES PREP TIME / 15 MINUTES COOKING TIME

1 tablespoon butter
2.5 oz dried porcini
1¾ cups chicken broth
¾ cup crème fraîche
Salt and freshly ground black pepper
4 cooked whole quail, stuffed with foie gras (ask your specialty grocer to do this)

Heat the butter in a skillet, add the porcini, and then gradually add the broth, letting the porcini absorb it completely before you add the next ladleful. Once the porcini are rehydrated and soft, add the crème fraîche and bring to a simmer over medium heat; cook a few minutes until the sauce thickens slightly, and season with salt and pepper. Serve the quail napped with the sauce.

Pages 228–229: Foie Gras–Stuffed Quail with Porcini Sauce; Porcini-Stuffed Cabbage Rolls

PORCINI RAVIOLI WITH PORCINI BUTTER ▶

SERVES 4 / 5 MINUTES PREP TIME (+ 1 HOUR SOAKING TIME) / 10 MINUTES COOKING TIME

1¾ oz dried porcini
4 tablespoons butter, at room temperature
1 lb porcini ravioli or tortellini (from an Italian specialty store)
2 tablespoons porcini bread crumbs (bread crumbs and a few dried porcini pulsed together in a food processor)

Soak the porcini in warm water for 1 hour. (Reserve the soaking liquid and add it to the pasta water when cooking the ravioli.) Squeeze out excess water from the porcini, chop them, and mix with the butter; set aside.

Cook the pasta in a mix of salted water and porcini soaking liquid.

Preheat the broiler. Divide the ravioli among four shallow ovenproof bowls, top with a portion of porcini butter and some porcini bread crumbs, and then broil for about a minute. Serve hot.

GRATIN OF BELGIAN ENDIVE AND PORCINI

SERVES 4 / 20 MINUTES PREP (+ 20 MINUTES SOAKING TIME) / 20 MINUTES COOKING TIME

1½ oz dried porcini
12 small heads Belgian endive
2 tablespoons butter
1 pinch sugar
½ lb sliced cooked ham, cut into strips
½ cup grated Emmenthal or Gruyère cheese
1 recipe Porcini Béchamel (recipe follows)

Soak the porcini in warm water for 20 minutes; reserve the soaking liquid.

Blanch the endive in boiling water for 5 minutes. Drain well and brown them lightly in the butter with the sugar and 1 tablespoon of the porcini soaking water in a skillet over medium heat. When nicely browned, remove the endive. Roll each one in some strips of ham, and then tuck them into an ovenproof gratin pan or other baking dish.

Preheat the oven to 425°F. Drain the porcini, squeeze out extra moisture, chop them, and stir them and the grated cheese into the béchamel. Spoon the sauce evenly over the endive, bake in the oven for 15 minutes; switch to broiler heat and then broil for another 5 minutes. Serve hot.

PORCINI BÉCHAMEL

MAKES 4 CUPS / 10 MINUTES PREP TIME (+ OVERNIGHT INFUSION TIME) / 10 MINUTES COOKING TIME

1½ oz dried porcini
4 cups milk
6 tablespoons butter
½ cup all-purpose flour

Soak the porcini in the milk and refrigerate overnight. The next day, melt the butter in a saucepan over medium heat, add the flour all at once, and stir with a wooden spoon until the roux turns a light golden color.

Off the heat, strain the porcini from the infused milk, and whisk the milk into the roux (discard the porcini). Return the pan to the heat, and cook until the sauce thickens, stirring constantly. Store in an airtight container in the refrigerator for up to 2 days.

Making this sauce gives you the chance to make some awesome recipes.

VEAL SHANKS WITH PORCINI AND BEAUJOLAIS (AND VICE VERSA) ▶

SERVES 4 / 20 MINUTES PREP TIME (+ 1 HOUR SOAKING TIME) / 4 HOURS COOKING TIME

3½ oz dried porcini
4 veal shanks
1 tablespoon olive oil
¾ cup Beaujolais wine
A few bay leaves
Black peppercorns
1 carrot, cut in chunks
1 onion, cut in chunks
2 garlic cloves
4 cups veal stock
Salt and freshly ground black pepper
1 tablespoon butter

Soak the porcini in warm water for 1 hour. Drain them, squeeze out excess moisture, and reserve about 1 cup of the soaking water. Brown the veal shanks in the olive oil over medium-high heat, add the Beaujolais, and deglaze the pan; add the bay leaves, peppercorns, carrot, onion, and garlic. Cover the veal with the reserved mushroom soaking liquid and the veal stock. Season with salt and pepper. Cover the pot, decrease the heat to medium-low, and simmer until the veal is very tender, about 4 hours.

Remove the shanks from the pan and strain the cooking liquid. Sauté the porcini in butter and add the cooking liquid. Return the veal to the sauce and reheat for a few minutes, and then serve.

CRÈME BRÛLÉE WITH PORCINI AND FOIE GRAS

SERVES 8 / 10 MINUTES PREP TIME (+ OVERNIGHT INFUSION TIME) / 30 MINUTES COOKING TIME

1½ oz dried porcini
2 cups milk
2 cups heavy cream
7 oz foie gras (preferably goose, but duck will be fine)
10 egg yolks, lightly beaten
1 pinch salt
8 tablespoons sugar

Soak the porcini in the milk and mix the cream and foie gras in a blender and refrigerate both overnight. The next day, strain the milk and discard the porcini. Preheat the oven to 300°F. Add the egg yolks to the milk along with the foie-gras cream and salt. Divide the mixture among eight shallow ovenproof ramekins. Set the ramekins in a baking pan, add boiling water to halfway up the sides of the ramekins, and bake for 30 minutes. Remove from the oven and chill for 2 hours. Sprinkle the custards with the sugar and caramelize under the broiler. Serve immediately.

PORCINI ICE CREAM

MAKES 4 CUPS / 10 MINUTES PREP TIME (+ OVERNIGHT INFUSION TIME) / 10 MINUTES COOKING TIME / 15 MINUTES CHURNING TIME

1½ oz dried porcini
2 cups plus 2 tablespoons milk
¾ cup heavy cream
5 egg yolks
1 cup sugar
Chocolate sauce or caramel sauce, for serving

Soak the porcini in the milk and refrigerate overnight. The next day, strain the milk and discard the porcini. Mix the milk with the cream, egg yolks, and sugar. Put the mixture into the top of a double boiler, and cook over low heat, stirring constantly and gently, until the custard coats the back of a spoon (about 10 minutes). Chill. Pour the custard into an ice cream maker and churn for about 15 minutes. Freeze until serving, topped with chocolate sauce.

DRIED FAIRY RING MUSHROOMS

Fairy rings are rot-resistant mushrooms, and therefore easy to dry. Nonetheless, we still see quite a few mediocre dried fairy rings. The thin cap and the springy stem make it tricky to dry using harsher methods (sun-drying outside). It takes about 20 pounds of fresh fairy rings to make 1 pound of dried, which explains its high price.

CHOOSE: Look for specimens that have been properly dried, meaning they were picked fresh and immediately dried in a dehydrator or specially adapted oven.

REHYDRATE AND COOK: When they're dry, their hazelnut fragrance is concentrated and their texture, after rehydrating in some butter or broth, is identical to a fresh fairy ring—better, actually, because the flavor and fragrance are more intense.

RAZOR CLAMS AND FAIRY RINGS MARINIÈRE

SERVES 4 / 15 MINUTES PREP TIME / 10 MINUTES COOKING TIME

2 tablespoons unsalted butter
4 shallots, minced
1 garlic clove, chopped
1 large handful dried fairy ring mushrooms
1 bunch flat-leaf parsley, chopped
⅔ cup dry white wine
2 lb razor clams

Heat the butter in a deep skillet over medium-high heat, add the shallots and garlic, and sauté.

After 5 minutes, add the mushrooms, half the parsley, and half the wine. Cook over high heat until the liquid has almost completely reduced. Then add the rest of the wine and the clams, and cover. When the clams have opened, uncover the pan and cook for another minute to reduce the liquid a bit more. Finished by adding the rest of the parsley; serve right away.

FAIRY RING AND BLACK OLIVE PISSALADIÈRE ▶

SERVES 4 / 15 MINUTES PREP TIME / 2 HOURS, 20 MINUTES COOKING TIME

4½ lb sweet onions (such as Walla Walla or Vidalia)
2 cups plus 2 tablespoons olive oil
1 tablespoon Asian fish sauce (optional)
1 lb prepared bread dough or pizza dough
3.5 oz dried fairy ring mushrooms, rehydrated in warm water
1 handful oil-cured black olives
Sprigs of thyme, savory, or both

In this recipe, we don't use anchovies, as you would in a traditional pissaladière*, but rather we pump up the flavor of the onions by adding a type of fish sauce made from fermented anchovies.*

Slice the onions and cook them in a Dutch oven with the olive oil over very low heat until they're very soft, sweet, and nicely caramelized, about 2 hours, stirring occasionally, especially toward the end of cooking. Add a bit of water if the onions seem to be getting dry, and then add the fish sauce, if you like.

Preheat the oven to 400°F. Roll out the dough on parchment paper. Fold the mushrooms into the onions and spread them evenly over the dough. Distribute the olives and herbs over the pissaladière, and bake for about 20 minutes. Let cool slightly before serving. You can serve the pissaladière warm or cold.

 Page 238: Razor Clams and Fairy Rings Marinière

WHITE BEANS AND FAIRY RINGS

SERVES 4 / 20 MINUTES PREP TIME / 30 MINUTES COOKING TIME

4½ lb fresh small white shell beans (such as cannellini), or 10½ oz dried white beans
1 carrot
1 head green garlic
1 bunch spring onions, dark green tops trimmed
1 bunch mixed fresh herbs (thyme, savory, marjoram, etc.)
A few peppercorns
1½ oz dried fairy ring mushrooms or 14 oz fresh fairy rings
3 tablespoons butter
Salt

Shell the beans, put them in a large pot, and cover them with cool water. Add the carrot, garlic, spring onions, herbs, and peppercorns. Simmer over very low heat (don't let it actually boil) until the beans are fully tender (about 20 minutes, if using fresh). Meanwhile, rehydrate the dried mushrooms by simmering them over medium-low heat in 2 tablespoons of the butter in a small pan. Remove and discard the carrot and herbs from the beans, salt the beans lightly, add the mushrooms, and serve with a bit of the pot liquid. You can add the remaining butter right before serving—it's more than delicious!

DRIED MOREL MUSHROOMS

It's hard to find dried morels coming from countries that adore eating them fresh, such as France, but Chile, Argentina, and Turkey have become important exporters. The price for dried morels may seem high, but you only need about 1 oz per person.

CHOOSE: You'll find a wide range of quality in dried morels. The best are fairly large, between 1 and 2 inches, nicely shaped, and not dusty. The slightly smoky flavor and firm texture of a dried morel can be preferable to fresh morels, which are sometimes bland.

REHYDRATE AND COOK: The method is simple—warm water plus 1 hour soaking (rinse them first to remove any sand). Always save some of the soaking water, which is very fragrant, to use when you cook them, or to add to broths. Just about any recipe calling for fresh morels can be made with dried.

VEAL CHEEKS WITH MORELS
SERVES 4 / 30 MINUTES PREP TIME (+ 1 HOUR SOAKING TIME) / 2 HOURS, 10 MINUTES COOKING TIME

3 oz dried morels, rehydrated in warm water
8 trimmed veal cheeks
2 tablespoons clarified butter (see page 18)
Salt and freshly ground black pepper
⅓ cup white wine
6 large carrots, sliced
6 shallots, sliced
1 bouquet garni (fresh parsley, thyme, rosemary, wrapped up in a leek green)
1 garlic clove
2 cups veal stock
2 tablespoons butter

Wring out the morels and strain ¾ cup of the soaking liquid; set the morels and liquid aside. Brown the veal cheeks in the clarified butter over medium-high heat; season generously with salt and pepper, add the wine, 2 carrots, 2 shallots, the bouquet garni, and garlic. Decrease the heat to medium. Cover with the veal stock and the reserved soaking liquid, and let simmer 2 hours, covered, until the veal is very tender.

Take out the veal and strain the cooking liquid. If it's a bit thin, simmer to reduce. Brown the remaining carrots and shallots in the whole butter with the morels. Add back the cooking liquid and the veal and simmer for 10 minutes over low heat; adjust the seasoning before serving.

SAINT-MARCELLIN CHEESES WITH MORELS ▶
SERVES 4 / 10 MINUTES PREP TIME (+ 1 HOUR SOAKING TIME) / 10 MINUTES COOKING TIME

1½ oz dried morels, rehydrated in warm water
Bay leaf
1 tablespoon butter
⅓ cup white dessert wine (such as late-harvest Riesling, Sauternes, or Rivesaltes Ambré)
1¾ crème fraîche
4 Saint-Marcellin cheeses (not too runny), or other small, washed-rind cow's milk cheeses

Wring out the morels, strain the soaking liquid, and set it aside. Gently cook the morels and bay leaf in the butter for about 2 minutes. Add the wine, increase the heat to medium, and simmer until reduced by three-quarters. Add the soaking liquid, reduce again by three-quarters, and then add the crème fraîche. Decrease the heat to medium-low and simmer 10 minutes. Meanwhile, preheat the broiler. Put each cheese on a small ovenproof plate and broil for about 4 minutes. Finish by spooning the cream sauce over the cheeses before serving.

Page 245: Veal Cheeks with Morels

DRIED SHIITAKE MUSHROOMS

CHOOSE: While France, Belgium, the United Kingdom, and other Western countries produce fine fresh shiitakes, the majority of the dried shiitakes are exported to Japan, very often organic versions (sun-dried), both cultivated and semiwild (cultivation in a natural outdoor environment). The nutritional benefits of shiitakes are not lost by drying. The gastronomic benefits, such as they are, become smokier and firmer.

SHIITAKE CHOUCROUTE

SERVES 4 / 5 MINUTES PREP TIME (+ 1 HOUR SOAKING TIME) / 20 MINUTES COOKING TIME

3½ oz dried shiitakes
⅓ cup dry white wine
Salt

Deviate from the traditional recipe of sausage, carrots, potatoes, and hot sauerkraut by replacing the sauerkraut with rehydrated shiitakes that have been gently simmered in white wine and a little salt. That's it—easy but good.

SQUID STUFFED WITH DRIED SHIITAKES

SERVES 4 / 30 MINUTES PREP TIME (+ 1 HOUR SOAKING TIME) / 25 MINUTES COOKING TIME

4 squid, about ½ lb
12 dried shiitakes
3 tablespoons olive oil
2 cooked pig's feet
½ lb bulk sausage
2 slices bread, stale or fresh, torn into crumbs
2 sprigs flat-leaf parsley, chopped
Salt and freshly ground black pepper

VINAIGRETTE
Piment d'espelette or other fruity ground dried pepper
2 tablespoons balsamic vinegar
2 tablespoons olive oil
Salt and freshly ground pepper

Pull out the insides of each squid, extract and discard the quill, pull off the thin outer membrane, and rinse well. Pat dry and set aside.

Soak the shiitakes in water for 1 hour. Wring them out, cut into small dice, and then sauté them gently in 1 tablespoon of the olive oil.

Preheat an outdoor grill. Grill the pig's feet and remove the bones (there are around 36!), chop the meat, and then mix with the sausage, bread, parsley, and the diced mushrooms. Season well with salt and pepper. Stuff the squid with the mixture and close with a wooden toothpick. Sauté the stuffed squid over medium-high heat in the remaining 2 tablespoons olive oil.

FOR THE VINAIGRETTE: Whisk together the piment d'espelette, vinegar, and olive oil and season with salt and pepper. Serve the squid hot or warm with the spicy vinaigrette.

DRIED WOOD EAR MUSHROOMS

These small brown mushrooms flourish year-round on the branches (even dead ones) and trunks of elder trees. A wood ear is slightly dome-shaped, with a smooth, veined interior, much like the inside of a cat's ear. They are also called tree-ear, cloud-ear, or in some cultures, Judas-ear, because Judas was hung on an elder tree.

CHOOSE: Almost impossible to find in the fresh state, mostly because there's no demand for them (and perhaps for a reason—they are quite gelatinous) but they are available dried. China produces and dries them on a commercial scale. Those are the black mushroom that you'll see in so many Asian soups and salads. Artisan-dried wood ears are much more appealing and are becoming easier to find.

REHYDRATE AND COOK: The flavor is slightly iffy, but it's the crunchy texture that makes these great ingredients for certain recipes. Rehydrate for 20 to 40 minutes in cold water, or soak them directly in a syrup.

WOOD EAR MUSHROOMS WITH PINEAPPLE IN SYRUP
SERVES 4 / 15 MINUTES PREP TIME / 5 MINUTES COOKING TIME

4 cups water
¾ cup sugar
1 vanilla bean, split lengthwise, and seeds scraped out
1 small ripe pineapple, peeled and cut into small chunks
1 splash kirsch
1 small handful dried wood ear mushrooms

Make a syrup by bringing the water, sugar, and vanilla bean and seeds to a boil over high heat. Pour the hot syrup over the pineapple chunks. Refrigerate until chilled. Pour the kirsch over the pineapple and keep chilled. Soak the mushrooms in water for 20 minutes, wring them out, and fold into the pineapple to serve.

ELDERBERRY WINE AND WOOD EAR MUSHROOM SOUP
SERVES 4 / 15 MINUTES PREP TIME / 5 MINUTES COOKING TIME

1 handful dried wood ear mushrooms
An assortment of white fruit: white peaches, gooseberries, etc.
1 vanilla bean
2 cups elderberry wine (preferably white)

Soak the mushrooms in water for 20 minutes. Wash the fruit and cut the peaches into quarters. Split and scrape the vanilla bean and mix the seeds into the elderberry wine. Pour the wine over the mushrooms and fruit and serve very cold.

DRIED AGARIC, ENOKI, SHAGGY MANE, REISHI, ROYAL SUN, BLACK TRUMPET, AND CHANTERELLE MUSHROOMS

Any mushroom can be dried, and if the current trend continues, we'll probably see more and more varieties being dried commercially, especially the rare and endangered species that aren't possible to obtain in fresh form. Case in point would be the shaggy mane, which is extremely perishable and must be eaten within two hours of harvest, and of which the fragrance, once dried, smells like wild strawberries. Same with the reishi *(Ganoderma lucidum)*, inedible because it's rock-hard, but which has highly therapeutic propeties, much valued over the centuries. You can make an infusion from the dried mushroom. Ditto for the *Agaricus blazei*, or royal sun mushroom, cultivated in Brazil and reported to be extremely rich in immune-boosting compounds. And last but not least, certain African chanterelles (from old-growth forests in Burundi), or *Termitomyces*, the giant mushrooms that grow on termite mounds.

PORK ROAST WITH AGARIC MUSHROOMS

SERVES 4 / 20 MINUTES PREP TIME (+ 20 MINUTES SOAKING TIME) / 45 MINUTES COOKING TIME

1¾ oz dried agaric mushrooms, soaked and wrung out
3 tablespoons clarified butter (see page 18)
3½ oz thick-cut bacon, finely diced
1½ oz anchovies, minced
1 small boneless pork roast, 1⅓ to 1¾ lb

Sauté the mushrooms in 1 tablespoon of the clarified butter over medium-high heat for about 2 minutes. Chop the mushrooms and mix with the bacon and anchovies. With a long, sharp knife, butterfly the pork so that you can open it up, stuff it, and roll it up like a pinwheel (or ask your butcher to do this). Lay the pork out flat. Spread the mushroom mixture over the inside of the pork, roll it up, and tie with butcher's twine. Brown the roast in the remaining 2 tablespoons clarified butter, and then put it into a Dutch oven. Cover and cook over very low heat for about 40 minutes, turning the roast from time to time. Let the roast rest about 10 minutes before slicing and serving.

ENOKI CONFIT WITH MIRIN

SERVES 4 / 10 MINUTES PREP TIME (+ 20 MINUTES SOAKING TIME) / 5 MINUTES COOKING TIME

1½ oz dried enoki mushrooms
⅓ oz dried fairy ring mushrooms (optional)
1 tablespoon butter
⅓ cup mirin
Salt

Soak the enokis and the fairy rings (if using) in warm water for 20 minutes. Wring them out and sauté them in the butter over low heat for 5 minutes. Add the mirin, increase the heat just a bit, and cook until the liquid has reduced to a glaze. Season with salt before serving.

SHAGGY MANES WITH ENOKIS

SERVES 4 / 10 MINUTES PREP TIME / 5 MINUTES COOKING TIME

1½ oz dried shaggy mane mushrooms
2 bunches enoki mushrooms
2 tablespoons butter
A few ginkgo nuts or fresh shelled hazelnuts
Salt and freshly ground black pepper

Sauté the mushrooms in the butter over low heat (they will plump up as they cook), add the ginkgo nuts, season with salt and pepper, and let simmer about 2 minutes. Serve hot.

SHAGGY MANES WITH SAFFRON AND PINE NUTS

SERVES 4 / 10 MINUTES PREP TIME / 5 MINUTES COOKING TIME

2 tablespoons pine nuts
1½ oz dried shaggy mane mushrooms
2 tablespoons butter
4 tablespoons water
1 pinch saffron threads
Salt and freshly ground black pepper
1 lemon (optional)

Lightly toast the pine nuts in a dry skillet and set aside. Sauté the mushrooms in the butter over low heat (they will plump up as they cook), add the water and saffron, and cook over very low heat until the liquid is completely reduced. Season with salt and pepper.

Serve with the pine nuts and, if you like, a squeeze of lemon.

MUSHROOM TEA

FOR ONE POT OF TEA / 5 MINUTES PREP TIME / 4 MINUTES INFUSION TIME

1 tablespoon slices dried reishi mushrooms
½ tablespoon slices dried shiitake mushrooms
½ tablespoon oolong tea leaves

Add the mushrooms and the tea leaves to the teapot. Pour simmering water into the pot and leave to steep 4 minutes before serving.

BLACK TRUMPET MUSHROOMS WITH OLIVES AND SMOKED PAPRIKA

SERVES 4 / 5 MINUTES PREP TIME (+ 1 HOUR SOAKING TIME) / 15 MINUTES COOKING TIME

3 oz dried black trumpet mushrooms
2 tablespoons olive oil
2 tablespoons chopped good quality black olives
1 tablespoon smoked paprika

Soak the mushrooms in lukewarm water for 1 hour. Wring them out and discard the soaking water. Sauté the mushrooms in the olive oil over low heat for 10 minutes, and then add the olives and paprika and continue cooking for another 5 minutes. Serve hot.

TWICE-BAKED POTATOES AND CHANTERELLES

SERVES 4 / 15 MINUTES PREP TIME (+ 1 HOUR SOAKING TIME) / 45 MINUTES COOKING TIME

3½ oz dried chanterelle mushrooms
4 large Yukon gold or other medium-starch potatoes
4 tablespoons melted butter
2 oz Beaufort, Comté, or Gruyère cheese
2 sprigs flat-leaf parsley, chopped
Freshly grated nutmeg
Salt and freshly ground black pepper

Soak the mushrooms in lukewarm water for 1 hour. Meanwhile, preheat the oven to 400°F. Wrap the potatoes in aluminium foil and bake until completely tender, about 40 minutes. Wring out the mushrooms and reserve about ½ cup of the soaking liquid. Sauté the mushrooms in half of the butter over medium heat.

Remove the potatoes from the oven, and preheat the broiler. When the potatoes are cool enough to handle, scoop out the flesh from the skins, keeping the skins intact. Mix the potato with the cheese, parsley, sautéed mushrooms, and a pinch of freshly grated nutmeg; season with salt and pepper. Pile the mixture back into the potato skins, drizzle with the rest of the melted butter, and broil for 2 minutes. Serve hot.

ROAST CHICKEN WITH ROYAL SUN MUSHROOMS

SERVES 4 / 10 MINUTES PREP TIME (+ 2 HOURS SOAKING TIME) / 40 MINUTES COOKING TIME

3.5 oz dried royal sun mushrooms
1 organic chicken, 2 to 3 lb
Salt and freshly ground black pepper
2 tablespoons butter

Soak the mushrooms in water for 2 hours. Preheat the oven to 350°F. Season the chicken generously with salt and pepper and roast the chicken for about 40 minutes (or until the juice runs clear when you poke the chicken just below the thigh with the tip of a knife). Meanwhile, drain the mushrooms, reserving a bit of the soaking water, then sauté the mushrooms in a skillet with the butter over medium heat for 20 minutes, adding a little bit of the soaking water during cooking to keep the mushrooms from drying out. When the chicken is cooked, strain off the pan juices and add ½ cup to the mushrooms. Carve the chicken and serve with the sautéed mushrooms.

Pages 254–255: Black Trumpet Mushrooms with Olives and Smoked Paprika; Twice-Baked Potatoes and Chanterelles

ALL THAT GLITTERS IS NOT GOLD

We've put together a selection of mushroom-based products, especially truffle-based ones, that we use sometimes. Some are house-made and others are store-bought. Be aware, however, that not all truffle products on the market are the best quality, so be a savvy buyer.

❶ **TRUFFLED SPIRITS.** An excellent way to use truffle trimmings (though only from black truffles). Your choice of alcohol, as long as it's good quality + black truffle + 3 months aging time. The best combinations are a matter of "what grows together, goes together": Armagnac or cognac with black truffles from Perigord, grappa from Barolo for truffles from Piedmont, for example. But you can play around with whatever combos sound good to you—nocino and truffle, smoked vodka, peaty whiskey.

❷ **TRUFFLE SALT.** Ingredients: sea salt, summer truffle *(Tuber aestivum)*, flavor. Truffle-based products rarely actually contain any black truffle *(Tuber melanosporum)*, and almost all use synthetic fragrance. Here, the truffle flecks are purely decorative.

❸ **TRUFFLED EGGS.** This is a great trick to maximize your investment in truffles: keep them for 2 days in a closed jar with some fresh eggs. The egg shell is porous and the scent of the black truffle is intense. You've got a truffle-flavored omelet!

❹ **TRUFFLED CHEESE.** Usually a type of young pecorino that's studded with summer truffles. It's only good when melted, and as the cheese ages, the flavor and fragrance fade.

❺ **TARTUFATA.** You'll find a lot of versions of this, but all share a base of cultivated mushrooms, truffle (summer or a small white summer variety called bianchetti), artificial flavor, and olive oil. The subtle differences depend on whether the spread contains black olives or anchovies or both. You can use this as you would pesto or tapenade, or as the base for a vinaigrette.

❻ **TRUFFLE JUICE.** Ingredients: water, black truffle *(Tuber melanosporum)*, salt. This product, which is expensive and mostly used in top restaurants, is only worth it if it contains real black truffles. But for the most part, you find truffle juice made with low-grade truffles destined for canning, which are in fact natural but not very complex. Truffle juice is used in sauces (such as *sauce périgourdine*), consommés, and stews (such as Osso Buco with Truffles, page 178).

❼ **HONEY WITH WHITE TRUFFLES.** Ingredients: honey, truffle *(Tuber albidum pico)*, olive oil, salt, flavoring. This is a strange recipe that uses the bianchetti, also called "poor man's truffle," which is a bit of a fraud. Nonetheless the honey is interesting in glazes and desserts.

❽ **MUSHROOM POWDERS.** Ingredients: dried mushrooms plus any spices you'd like. You can make the base yourself by processing dried mushrooms in a powerful blender or food processor or grinding them with a mortar and pestle. Then add the spices you want (see page 265). The resulting powder is a great flavor booster.

❾ **PORCINI SALT.** Ingredients: coarse sea salt, dried porcini. Here again, you can adapt the recipe to suit your taste by creating your own mix of mushrooms. Use it to season salads, flavor pastas, and more.

②

④

6

7

8

9

RECIPES BASED ON PRODUCTS DERIVED FROM MUSHROOMS

GLAZED PORK BELLY WITH TRUFFLED HONEY

SERVES 4 / 20 MINUTES PREP TIME / 1 HOUR COOKING TIME

1½ lb pork belly
¾ cup white wine
1 garlic clove
A few bay leaves
Black peppercorns
4 tablespoons truffled honey

Preheat the oven to 350°F. Brown the pork belly in a Dutch oven or heavy pot over medium-high heat, making sure to brown all sides. Add the wine, garlic, bay leaves, and 6 or 7 peppercorns. Put the pot in the oven, uncovered, and cook for 1 hour. Add a little water if the wine cooks off and the pot becomes dry. When the pork is very tender and fully cooked, take it from the oven and pour off the pan juices into a bowl. Skim off the fat and mix the remaining juices with the honey. Put the pot on low heat and glaze the pork by basting frequently with the honey mixture. Serve hot.

◀ ## ARTICHOKES CAMUS WITH TRUFFLE TAPENADE

SERVES 4 / 15 MINUTES PREP TIME / 45 MINUTES COOKING TIME

4 artichokes, trimmed
Juice of 2 lemons
3 tablespoons olive oil
3 tablespoons balsamic vinegar
6 tablespoons tartufata

Cook the artichokes for about 45 minutes in boiling water that has the lemon juice squeezed into it. You'll know the artichokes are done when you can easily pull off a leaf. Chill, and when cool enough to handle, pull off the leaves and arrange them on a platter, and then scrape the choke from the artichoke bottoms and place them in the center of the platter. Mix together the olive oil, vinegar, and tartufata, and dress the artichokes. Serve slightly warm or chilled.

PASTA SHELLS WITH TRUFFLED CHEESE

SERVES 4 / 15 MINUTES PREP TIME / 25 MINUTES COOKING TIME

2 cups dried pasta shells
1¾ cups marinara or other basic tomato sauce
5 oz truffled cheese, cut into small bits
1 small truffle, for garnish (optional)

Cook the pasta in boiling salted water until it's al dente. Heat the marinara sauce in a saucepan over medium-high heat for a few minutes to thicken it.

Preheat the oven to 425°F. Spread the sauce in the bottom of four small ovenproof gratin dishes or shallow ramekins. Fill each pasta shell with a bit of cheese. Arrange the shells in the gratin dishes, put the dishes in the oven, and bake until the cheese is completely melted. Turn the oven to broil and broil for another 5 minutes. Serve hot, with some truffle shaved on top, if you like.

MUSHROOM POWDERS

Grind to a powder and mix

¾ oz dried black trumpet mushrooms, 1 whole clove, 4 black peppercorns
For beef cheeks braised in red wine, for a roast chicken

¾ oz dried morels, 1 big pinch oolong tea leaves
For a sauce, a stew, steamed clams

¾ oz dried porcini, ¾ oz preserved lemon rind, 1 large pinch coarse salt
To season white-fleshed fish, sea scallops, raw porcini slices

¾ oz dried porcini, ½ oz gomasio (sesame salt), 1 large pinch dried shrimp
To season rice or a salad

¾ oz dried fairy rings, ¾ oz hazelnuts, ½ tablespoon coarse salt
To season a veal chop or potatoes

¾ oz dried shiitakes, 2 tablespoons wakame seaweed
To make a broth, for soba noodles, for seafood, for fingerling potatoes

PRESERVES

Chanterelle Vodka

SHIITAKES IN VINEGAR

Cut and discard the stems from **2 lb shiitakes**. Spread out the caps on a baking sheet or counter and cover them with **coarse salt** for 2 hours.

Rinse and wring out any moisture. Fill a sterile canning jar with the mushrooms. Heat **2 cups vinegar**, add **1 whole clove**, a few **black peppercorns**, and some **juniper berries**. Pour the hot vinegar over the mushrooms. Seal your canning jars following proper canning procedure. Let rest for 1 month before using.

GRILLED WHITE MUSHROOMS IN OIL

Grill **4½ lb of lightly oiled white mushrooms**, either on an outdoor grill or under the broiler. When they're nicely browned, put them in a large sterile canning jar and cover with **good-quality olive oil or canola oil** enhanced with **1 garlic clove, 1 small hot chile**, and a few **bay leaves**. Refrigerate and let rest for 1 week before using.

FIELD AGARIC PICKLES

Boil **4½ lb mushrooms** with water to cover for 2 minutes. Drain well and put them in a large sterile canning jar, cover with **good vinegar** enhanced with a pinch of nice **salt**, some **whole fennel seeds**, and **1 sprig fresh tarragon**. Let rest for 15 days before using.

BLACK POPLAR MUSHROOMS IN WHITE WINE

Boil **2 lb black poplar mushrooms** in water to cover for 1 minute. Drain well and put them in a sterile canning jar with a few **bay leaves**.

Heat **3 cups white wine** with a few **black peppercorns, juniper berries**, and **1 whole clove**. Pour the hot mixture over the mushrooms. Let rest for 2 days before using.

CANDIED CHANTERELLES

Cook **1¼ lb cleaned chanterelles** in a **simple syrup** (1 part sugar to 1 part water) for about 10 minutes. Keep simmering the mushrooms in the syrup until they become translucent and nicely candied.

Store in the syrup in an airtight container in the refrigerator for up to 2 weeks.

◀ PARASOL MUSHROOMS IN OIL

Select **20 nice young parasol mushrooms**. Boil them in a mixture of **salted water** and **white wine or cider vinegar** for 5 minutes, skimming off any foam that rises. Remove from the water and transfer to a sterile canning jar. Cover with **olive oil**, seal tightly, and let rest in the refrigerator a few days before using.

Pages 270–273: Grilled White Mushrooms in Oil; Shiitakes in Vinegar; Field Agaric Pickles; Black Poplar Mushrooms in White Wine

LE SPORT
C'EST BIEN
LES SPORES
C'EST MIEU
POUR LA
RÉINTRODUCTION
DE LA
ESCE DE LOUP
ANS LE VERCORS !
LA MYCOLOGIE
A
L'ACADÉMIE
TOUS
A
LA POÊLE !
OUR
L'AGARIC
DES
TROTTOIRS !

FEATURING

Cédric, guitarist and chef

Joël, ex-chef of Café des Spores

Philippe, team leader and author

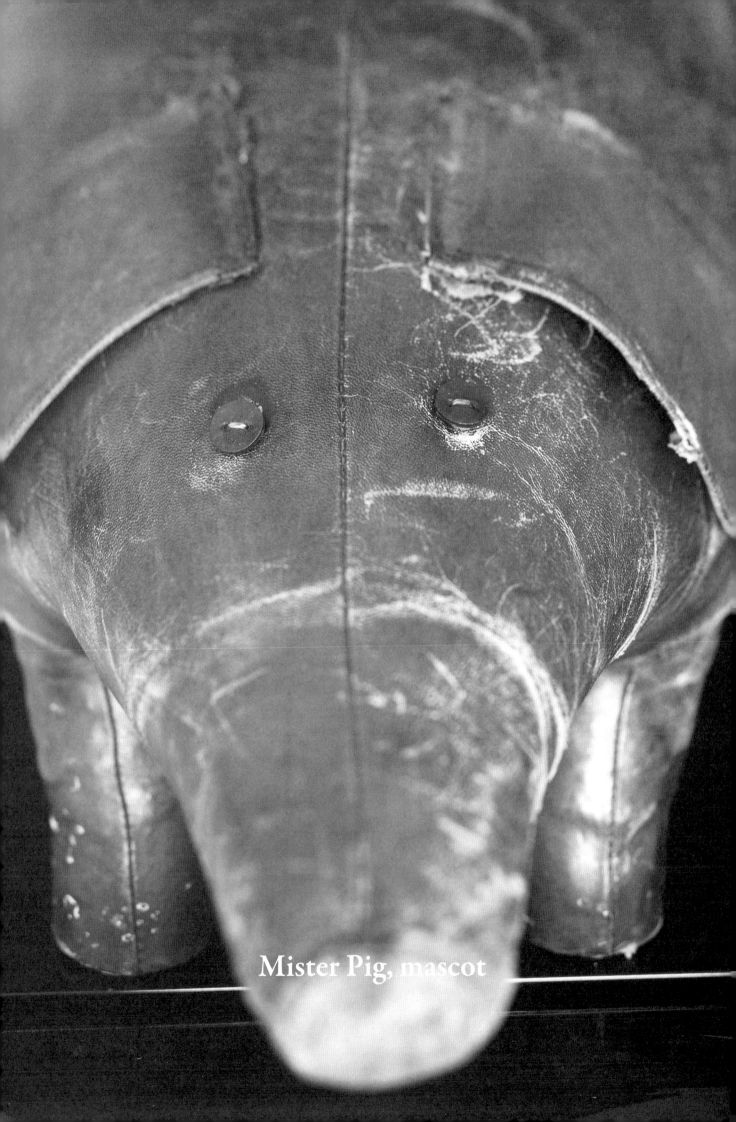

Mister Pig, mascot

Frédéric, photographer

Pierrick, designer

INDEX

BIBLIOGRAPHY

GENERAL FOOD

Alain Tardif – *La Mycothérapie* – Amyris – 2007
Jill Fullerton – *The Truth About Food* – Bloomsbury – 2007
Dr L. Chevalier – *Impostures et Vérités sur les aliments* – Fayard – 2007
collectif – *L'Avenir de la truffe face au réchauffement climatique* – Albin Michel – 2008
Peter Atkins – *Le Parfum de la fraise* – Dunod – 2004

MUSHROOM COOKERY

Antonio Carluccio – *Complete Mushroom Book: The Quiet Hunt* – Günd – 2003
Dr Paul Ramain – *Mycogastronomie* – Jeanne Laffite – 1953
Régis Marcon – *Ma Cusine des champignons* – Calmann-Lévy – 2001
Jean-Claude Ferrero – *Champignons* – Éd. du Chêne – 2001
Lucien Vanel – *Saveurs et humeurs* – Éd. Daniel Briand – 1990
R. B. Courtine – *La Cuisine des terroirs* – Renaissance du livre – 1998
Jaunautt & Brillet – *La Cuisine des champignons* – Ouest-France – 1997
Patrik Jaros – *La Truffe* – Taschen – 1998
Petras Ribas, Llorenç – *La millor cuina dels bolets* – Empuries – 2000
A. Oshima – K.J. Cwiertka – *Kaiseki Recipes* – Stichting Kunstboek – 2006
Giorgio Locatelli – *Made In Italy* – Fourth Estate – 2008
S. Alexander & M. Beer – *Saveurs de Toscane* – Ullmann – 2007
Antoinette Sturbelle – *Mes Recettes ont une histoire* – ACTES SUD – 2007

GUIDES AND REFERENCES

Champignons – Nathan – coll. « Miniguide tout terrain » – 2009
Renate Volk – *Champignons* – Ulmer – 2003
Yvon Leclerc – *Champignons comestibles* – Broquet – 2001
J.-M. Polese – *Bolets, cèpes et girolles* – Artémis – 2001
M. Locquin – *Les Champignons* – PUF – coll. « Que sais-je » – 2001
Mirko Svrcek – *Les Champignons* – Marabout – 1975
M. Cayla – *Les Champignons insolites* – Chiron – 1997
C. Epinat & P. Starosta – *Champignons* – Éd. du Chêne – 1998
J.-M. Olivier, P. Sourzat, J. C. Savignac – *Truffe et Trufficulture* – Fanlac – 2002
Jean Guillot, Hervé Chaumeton, Gerard Germain – *Les champignons et les termes de mycologie* – Nathan – 1993